Bluffer's®

GUIDE TO

BREXIT

BORIS STARLING

© Haynes Publishing 2018
Published June 2018

All rights reserved. No part of this publication
may be reproduced, stored in a retrieval system
or transmitted in any form or by any means, electronic,
mechanical, photocopying, recording or otherwise,
without the prior permission from Haynes Publishing.

A CIP Catalogue record for this book
is available from the British Library.

ISBN: 978 1 78521 218 5

Library of Congress control no. 2018932896

Published by Haynes Publishing,
Sparkford, Yeovil, Somerset BA22 7JJ
Tel: 01963 440635
Int. tel: +44 1963 440635
Website: www.haynes.com

Printed in Malaysia.

Bluffer's Guide®, Bluffer's® and Bluff Your Way®
are registered trademarks.

Series Editor: David Allsop.
Front cover illustration by Alan Capel.

CONTENTS

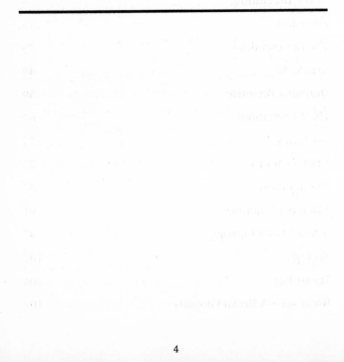

'I think that the people of this country have had enough of experts.'

Michael Gove

BREXISTENTIAL MATTERS

There are few, if any, subjects better suited to the noble art of bluffing than Brexit.

Firstly, it's the dominant political issue of our age. Brexit consumes most of the government's bandwidth, and most of the political news coverage. Heck, it's probably the most dominant political issue of any age within living memory. You may like to opine (for the true bluffer always has one eye on history) that the country has not been so split since 1642, when parliamentarians and royalists styled themselves Roundheads and Cavaliers respectively and fought a nine-year civil war. Like Brexit, that conflict was preceded by a constitutional crisis in Scotland: like Brexit, the issue of sovereignty was of paramount importance; and like Brexit, the role of parliament was also crucial.

Second, everyone has an opinion on Brexit. This is not a debate for the neutral. Brexit is tribal (more on this later). If Brexit was a sporting rivalry, it would be Rangers vs. Celtic, India vs. Pakistan, Real Madrid vs. Barcelona, Ali vs. Frazier. Whatever you say, you can guarantee that half the people are going to agree with you and the other half are going to tell you you're mistaken (though they may put it more trenchantly than that). Either way, you will be called into action.

And finally, no-one really has a clue what's going on. Oh, they *think* they do, and they will certainly *tell* you they do. You will, for example, come across people who insist in sonorous tones that we are heading serenely towards sunlit uplands, and who will repeat this assurance no matter what they're asked. These people are called Cabinet ministers.

Conversely, if you read warnings that the whole process is a farce and that Britain will soon be a post-apocalyptic wasteland, you are almost certainly on the *Guardian* website. Both these outcomes cannot be true. It may be that neither of them ends up being true. Brexit will rumble on for years, and no-one can predict the result for sure, as it depends on so many factors which are both individually and collectively unquantifiable. The effects are, at best, only just starting to be felt.

In this absence of certainty lies the bluffer's natural habitat. The guiding principle of Bluffing, and the *raison d'être* of the Bluffer's Guides (now entering their fifth decade of imparting instant wit and wisdom) is that a little knowledge is a desirable thing. Since that is all most of us are ever going to have anyway, we might as well get to know how to spread it thinly but effectively (like Marmite, or Gentleman's Relish, or Sandwich Spread, or indeed any other significant British contribution to world gastronomy, all of which are best applied sparingly).

Careful manipulation of some rudimentary facts will help you bluff your way through with a reasonable degree of nonchalance. This is especially important in these heady days of instant online information: when everyone has Google literally at their fingertips, failure to polish your bluffing techniques will leave you at a social and professional disadvantage.

This book is therefore not a 'How To' guide, but rather a 'How To Pretend You Know How To' guide. (There is a subtle distinction.) It's not about being an expert, as Mr Gove would tell you. It is certainly not a comprehensive Brexit primer, as one of those would run to 10,000 pages and be the kind of insomnia cure for which Big Pharma would pay billions.[1] As the Bluffer's Guides strapline reads: 'It's not what you know, it's what they think you know.'

This book gives the basics of Brexit: the history behind Britain's relationship with Europe, the referendum itself and the way it divided (and continues to divide) this country, the legalities of the split, and some of the areas which will be most affected. It drops in a few French, Latin and Greek terms, which you should use judiciously in order to give you that certain *je ne sais quoi* (there's another one for free).

So come in hard, drop some esoteric facts, make a few opaque allusions, and with any luck your interlocutors will think you have the kind of inside knowledge usually confined to the most senior civil servants. If in doubt, ask yourself: what would Bruce Willis do? He'd bluff hard. He'd bluff harder. And when all else failed, he'd bluff hard with a vengeance.

Be like Bruce.

---

1   Memo to self: ring agent with that idea immediately after finishing this.

ß

Jim Hacker: *Brussels is a shambles. You know what they say about the average Common Market official? He has the organising ability of the Italians, the flexibility of the Germans and the modesty of the French. And that's topped up by the imagination of the Belgians, the generosity of the Dutch and the intelligence of the Irish.*

Yes, Minister

IN THE BREGINNING

The United Kingdom (that is, Great Britain (England, Scotland and Wales) and Northern Ireland) voted on 23 June 2016 to leave the European Union (EU), a departure which is scheduled for 29 March 2019 but is unlikely to effectively happen until 31 December 2020.

The EU is a political and economic union which comprises 28 countries. In order of accession, these countries are:

- the six founder members of what was then the European Economic Community (EEC) in 1957: Belgium, France, Italy, Luxembourg, the Netherlands and West Germany
- Denmark, Ireland and the UK, in 1973
- Greece, in 1981
- Portugal and Spain, in 1986
- Austria, Finland and Sweden, in 1995
- Czech Republic, Cyprus, Estonia, Hungary, Latvia, Lithuania, Malta, Poland, Slovakia and Slovenia, in 2004

- Bulgaria and Romania, in 2007
- Croatia, in 2013.

The UK is the first country to have signalled its intention to leave the EU once already a member, though the Norwegian people have twice turned down accession (in referendums) despite their country having been offered admission.

The EU has its own parliament and governmental structures. It also has its own currency, the euro, though adoption of this is not compulsory: only 19 of the 28 member states are currently members of the eurozone. Bulgaria, Croatia, Czech Republic, Denmark, Hungary, Poland, Romania, Sweden, and of course the UK are the holdouts, though of these Denmark is the only one (apart from the UK) legally exempt from ever having to use the euro: all the others have pledged to do so when their economies meet the criteria for entry into the eurozone.

The EU began as the EEC, better known as the Common Market, and the single market – a zone encompassing all member states – is still at the heart of what the EU means. The single market in turn is predicated on 'four freedoms' – the freedom of movement of people, goods, services and capital. These principles aim to create a continent without internal borders, more or less, where trade barriers are removed and regulations harmonised across the union, so that a butcher in Manchester can do business in Madrid, Munich or Milan as easily as he can in Milton Keynes.

1. *free movement of people*. This is, at least in the UK, the most controversial of the four freedoms, and was at the heart of the immigration debate. Under free movement of people, any EU citizen has the right to live and work in any EU country.

2. *free movement of goods*. With no customs duties or other trade barriers, goods can move as freely within the EU as they can within a constituent nation. Tariffs are imposed on imports from outside the EU, and all EU members must adhere to these tariffs: any external trade deal is negotiated by the EU rather than by individual countries. Any goods imported from outside the EU, subject of course to applicable tariffs, can then circulate freely within the EU. Free movement of goods is crucial in an era of 'just-in-time' delivery and integrated supply chains, where even minor delays can cause major knock-on problems.

3. *free movement of services*. Any EU company can establish an office in another EU country and provide services in that country. Services account for more than two-thirds of all economic activity within the EU.

4. *free movement of capital*. This allows capital and payments to be transferred freely and without restriction within the union. These include things like buying currency, buying real estate, issuing and receiving company shares and loans, opening bank accounts, and so on.

'We have our own dream and our own task. We are with Europe, but not of it. We are linked but not combined. We are interested and associated but not absorbed.'

Winston Churchill, 1930.

BREVISION

1945–1973

It's impossible to understand Brexit without first understanding a little of Britain's recent history with Europe ('recent' in this instance meaning 'postwar', in the kind of way your grandfather will use the phrase 'the other day' to mean '1972'.) And nothing becomes the bluffer like a judicious bit of historical analysis.

All those old government communiqués in what was once the Public Record Office and is now the National Archives (the title changed in 2003, something the bluffer should know if only because it suggests long periods spent studying dusty tomes) clearly show the confusion in both the Attlee and Churchill administrations about Britain's place in the world.

On one side of the triangle, Britain had France and Germany begging it – sometimes almost literally – to come into the European project with them as a central triumvirate. On the second side of the triangle was the Commonwealth rising from the embers of a rapidly vanishing empire (India, the 'jewel in the crown', had become independent in 1947, and other colonies were agitating to follow suit), and on the third was the USA and the 'special relationship'.

What did the British do? They vacillated. Very British. They almost certainly chatted about the weather too and kept offering people tea. Gradually the Commonwealth became best known for hosting an Olympics-lite every four years and for receptions at Buckingham Palace where officials prayed that Prince Philip wouldn't say anything too racist and the Queen asked various dictators whether they'd come far.

The special relationship between London and Washington has waxed and waned over the decades, depending not just on the personalities of those in power at the time but also on the fact that Britain and America are fundamentally different countries. The issues which vex many Americans – gun control, religion, abortion – simply don't register for many Britons (or indeed for many Europeans).

And having stayed out of Europe when the Europeans asked them in, the British are now leaving when they're being asked to stay. National schizophrenia or a unique nation sure of its unique place in the world? Or, as so often with Brexit, a bit of both? This the kind of existential question which the skilled bluffer can pose before discreetly stepping back from the conversational fray, allowing everyone else to display varying degrees of ignorance while the Bluffer's own magisterial sageness remains intact.

Although many Britons count themselves as

Europhiles or citizens of the continent, the country has never had a strong pro-European movement like the ones founded in western continental Europe after the war. A pan-European structure was seen as desirable to maintain a peace shattered twice in the previous three decades. Germany, riven with guilt following the end of the Third Reich, uncomplainingly acquiesced: those nations that the Nazis had occupied were equally keen to be part of any organisation aimed at ensuring no repeat of that. But Britain, the island nation which had escaped invasion, did not have the same psychological scars.

So Britain chose not to be among the founder members of the European Communities. Instead, it was the 'Inner Six' – West Germany, France, Belgium, the Netherlands, Luxembourg and Italy, the latter five all having been forced to endure German troops on their soil during World War Two – who formed first the European Coal and Steel Community (ECSC) in 1951 and then the European Atomic Energy Community (Euratom) and the European Economic Community (EEC) in 1957.

The EEC, also known as the Common Market, was much the largest and best-known of the three. Britain did in fact apply to join, first in 1961 and then again in 1967, but on both occasions the application was vetoed by French President Charles de Gaulle, who said that the UK *'is insular, she is maritime, she is linked through her exchanges, her markets, her supply lines to the most diverse and often the most distant countries; she pursues essentially industrial and commercial activities, and only slight agricultural ones. She has in all her doings very marked and very original habits and traditions. In short, the nature, the structure, the very situation that are England's differ profoundly from those of the continentals.'*

It's striking how similar de Gaulle's rationale for keeping the UK out of the EEC in the 1960s was to the Leave campaign's rationale for taking the UK out of the EU half a century later. Was de Gaulle the first UKIPper? Though knowing de Gaulle, he could also have used his veto because:

a. He was still a bit peeved at being sidelined by Churchill before, during, and after D-Day

b. he feared that British entry would be a Trojan horse for American influence in the EEC

c. he was still smarting over the way Britain had behaved during the Suez affair in 1956

d. he thought Britain would unbalance the Franco-German axis at the heart of the EEC

e. he was feeling particularly obstreperous that day

f. all of the above.

1973–1992

De Gaulle's successor as French President, Georges Pompidou, proved more reasonable (not a particularly arduous task, granted), and the UK joined the Common Market in 1973. Two years later, a referendum on whether to stay in the EEC – the first ever national referendum held in the UK – saw more than two-thirds vote in favour of remaining.

Even a quick look at the campaign for that 1975 referendum shows how different the political landscape was back then, when tweets were what birds made and facebooks were collections of criminal mugshots. There were no televised leader debates, there was a more respectful and deferential tone towards the men and women making their cases (Ted Heath, Shirley Williams, Roy Jenkins, Tony Benn, Enoch Powell and so on), and broadcasters made arguably greater attempts to educate voters as to how the EEC (as it was then) worked (ITN made 18 three-minute films explaining various features of the Common Market, for example).

It is simplistic but probably broadly true to say that most Britons would have been happy for European integration to remain at the level of the single market they had resoundingly endorsed in that referendum. When Labour leader Michael Foot campaigned in the 1983 general election on a commitment to withdraw from the EEC, his party was trounced (though there were many other reasons for that, not least Margaret Thatcher's triumph in the Falklands War the previous year, Labour's commitment to unilateral nuclear disarmament at a time of heightened Cold War tension, and of course the 'donkey jacket' he wore at the Cenotaph on Remembrance Day in 1981 which cemented his popular image as Worzel Gummidge (even though it was actually a duffel coat).[2]

But European integration was continuing, both vertically (ever-increasing political union) and horizontally (a long-term project to bring the former Warsaw Pact countries of eastern Europe into the fold after the fall of the Berlin Wall in 1989). Every step towards such closer integration sat uneasily not just with an island race but also – especially – with the Conservative Party. (There is some truth to the argument that the 2016 Brexit referendum was effectively an internecine Tory war played out on the national stage). Ever since Thatcher was deposed in 1990, Conservative divisions over Europe have bubbled under, and occasionally bubbled over.

'We went into the ERM in despair and left in disgrace.'

- Sir Alan Budd, former chief economic adviser to the Treasury.

1992–2015

1992 was a seismic year for Britain's relationship with the EU. It was the year of the Maastricht Treaty, the greatest single leap forward for pan-European political

---

2   Foot's fellow Labour MP Walter Johnson said the coat made him look 'like an out-of-work Irish navvy.' The Queen Mother, on the other hand, told Foot that it was 'a sensible coat for a day like this.'

unity: the treaty's provisions included common policies for foreign affairs, security and justice, and also set out criteria for a single currency (the euro).

It was also the year in which the UK withdrew from the European Exchange Rate Mechanism (ERM), which had pegged sterling to the Deutschmark, after currency speculators had set the pound plunging and interest rates spiralling on 'Black Wednesday'. The cost to the taxpayer of sorting this out was more than £3bn.[3]

Two years later, Anglo-French billionaire Sir James Goldsmith founded the Referendum Party, whose sole aim was to force a referendum on the question 'Do you want the United Kingdom to be part of a federal Europe or do you want the United Kingdom to return to an association of sovereign nations that are part of a common trading market?'[4]

The Referendum Party won 2.6% of votes (but no seats) in the 1997 general election, and disbanded after Goldsmith's death later that year.[5] However, the party's brief flourishing had shown there *was* an appetite for an avowedly Eurosceptic party. In the early 2000s, the UK

---

3   Fun fact: Norman Lamont was Chancellor of the Exchequer on Black Wednesday. The pictures of him talking to journalists on that frantic day show a figure in the background: his special adviser, a fresh-faced chap. Name of David Cameron. Wonder what became of him?

4   As questions go, it could have been snappier, let's face it. It doesn't exactly have the pzazz of 'to be or not to be', for example.

5   Goldsmith himself had stood in Putney against David Mellor, and the two had traded insults at the election count (though even that had been overshadowed by Michael Portillo losing his seat in Enfield Southgate, only to return to our television screens some years later clad in the most terrifying array of pastel-coloured clothes since *Miami Vice*.)

Independence Party (UKIP), which had actually been founded a year before the Referendum Party but had been overshadowed and outspent by it, began making headway of its own – not least in reaction to two major events in European integration.

The first was the introduction of the euro to general circulation in 2002: it was no coincidence that UKIP included the sterling sign in its party logo. The second was the changing centre of EU gravity. Many adjectives are used to describe the EU, but 'daring' is rarely one. Grey men in grey suits do not do 'daring'. But how else to describe the events of 1 May 2004 when, like a nightclub bouncer suddenly throwing aside the rope, the EU admitted ten countries in one go?

In one fell swoop, this changed the EU's entire character. Before, the EU had been a handful of developed countries focussed around the Franco-German axis, a strictly western European affair (Greece apart, and that itself would come home to roost during the Greek economic travails which began in 2009). Now came eight eastern European countries and two Mediterranean ones, and – at least for many of the original residents – there went the neighbourhood.

The union's richest country, Luxembourg, has five and a half times the per capita purchasing power of Bulgaria, the poorest. Germany accounts for a fifth of the union's GDP, Malta for less than a thousandth. Determined to peg 19 different economies, all with their own strengths and weaknesses, to a single currency?

Welcome to the eurozone crisis.

Taking advantage of growing British disquiet with all this, UKIP performed increasingly well in European Parliamentary elections, doubling its number of seats from 12 in 2004 to 24 in 2014.

It also had what every party dreams of – a leader guaranteed airtime and column inches. Nigel Farage was, and remains, nothing if not a Marmite politician.[6] You either love him or hate him, but either way his influence on the referendum was profound, especially for a man who had never won a Westminster seat, who served as a parliamentary member of an institution he wanted to destroy, and who wasn't even part of the official Leave campaign. It's hard to argue anything other, though of course the bluffer will leaven this with a sprinkling of nuance: 'of course, Farage is a fiercely

---

6   Former Wimbledon champion Goran Ivanisevic expounded the theory that there was not one Goran but three:

Good Goran, who won tennis matches and was amiably eccentric

Bad Goran, who had enormous tantrums and smashed rackets

Emergency Goran, who was summoned when 15-40 down on his own serve by mentally dialling 999, and who served four aces in a row to win the game before disappearing again.

By the same token, you could also make a case for three Nigels, with your own viewpoint responsible for whichever one came out on top:

Good Nigel: a hearty chap full of bonhomie and always up for a pint, a straight talker socking it to those dreary PC pinkos with some home truths.

Bad Nigel: a golf club bore with a braying laugh, the type of man who reckons that if he wears a blazer with gold buttons you might think he's commodore of the yacht club.

Emergency Nigel, who with a week before polling day unveils a poster which was widely seen as unrepentantly and shamelessly racist (harking back to David Cameron's description of UKIP as full of 'fruitcakes, loonies and closet racists'.)

Unlike Goran, however, Nigel doesn't eat the same meal in the same restaurant every night throughout Wimbledon, and nor does he relax before important events (speeches for him, tennis matches for Goran) by watching *Teletubbies*. Probably.

effective rabble rouser and a formidable debater, but by offering simple solutions to complex problems he risks perpetuating or even exacerbating those problems...'

It was UKIP's growing membership under Farage – including right-wing members of the Conservative Party who thought Cameron too liberal, what with his support for gay marriage and his photoshoots with Arctic huskies, and had therefore defected – which prompted Cameron to try and head off the UKIP threat. In January 2013, he promised that, if the Conservatives won the 2015 general election, the government would hold a referendum on whether or not to remain in the EU.

Whether or not Cameron thought he'd ever have to follow through on this promise, only he knows. He had needed the pro-EU Liberal Democrats to form a coalition government in 2010 – a coalition which had worked better than most people had predicted, and had at least lasted the course until 2015 – and, had he needed to form another coalition with them after 2015, they could have vetoed the referendum as the price of coalition.

But when the Conservatives won a slim, surprise overall majority of 12, the die was cast. The UK would have a referendum on Brexit. And it would make every other political debate seem like small beer in comparison.

Sir Humphrey Appleby: Minister, Britain has had the same foreign policy objective for at least the last 500 years: to create a disunited Europe. In that cause we have fought with the Dutch against the Spanish, with the Germans against the French, with the French and Italians against the Germans, and with the French against the Germans and Italians. Divide and rule, you see. Why should we change now, when it's worked so well?

Jim Hacker: That's all ancient history, surely?

Sir Humphrey: Yes, and current policy. We had to break the whole thing [the EEC] up, so we had to get inside. We tried to break it up from the outside, but that wouldn't work. Now that we're inside we can make a complete pig's breakfast of the whole thing: set the Germans against the French, the French against the Italians, the Italians against the Dutch... The Foreign Office is terribly pleased; it's just like old times.

Hacker: But surely we're all committed to the European ideal?

Sir Humphrey: [chuckles] Really, minister.

Yes, Minister

ℬ

'I don't think we should be given a vote. I see politicians on TV every night telling us that this is a f***ing momentous decision that could f***ing change Britain forever and blah, blah, blah. It's like, okay, why don't you f***ing do what we pay you to do which is run the f***ing country and make your f***ing mind up....What are you asking the people for? 99% of the people are thick as pigs**t.'

Noel Gallagher, June 2016.

THE BREFERENDUM

THE QUESTION AND THE PROVISIONS

In essence, a referendum on Britain's continued membership of the EU seems simple enough. But the legal status of the referendum, the issue of the exact majority required, and even the wording of the question itself would all play vital roles not just in the campaign but also after the plebiscite had been held. This was to prove the first rule of Brexit: the simpler something seemed, the more sources of argument it would provide.

Under the terms of the European Union Referendum Act, passed by 554 votes to 53 in the Commons the month after the 2015 general election, the referendum had to be held by the end of 2017. The bill specified plenty of things – campaign length, campaign spending, voter eligibility – but it did *not*:

- require the government to implement the results of the referendum
- set a time limit by which a vote to leave the EU should be implemented.

The referendum was therefore technically a consultative one, enabling the electorate to express an opinion but not legally binding the government to act on this opinion. (This is largely analogous to the 'technically consultative' question a wife may ask her husband – 'does my bum look big in this?' – where his answer may not be legally binding but can have serious consequences nonetheless.)

Given the magnitude of the issue and the ramifications of any vote to leave, many people thought that the government should not only have insisted that the result be legally binding, but should also have built in a requirement for a supermajority, most probably of 60% (three-fifths) or 66.6% (two-thirds). Supermajorities are relatively common practice across the world when major constitutional changes are at stake – Canada, India, Japan and the USA are some of the countries which use them – though the only supermajority provided for in the British constitution is the two-thirds of parliamentary approval needed for a general election outside the usual five-year term of the Fixed Parliaments Act.[7]

It was to be this lack of legal compulsion which many Remainers cited when the referendum went against them. 'Ah, but it wasn't binding.' To which Leavers replied by pointing at the government leaflet posted to every household five weeks before the referendum which

7   If you wish to know more about this please write to Mrs T. May in 10 Downing Street, London SW1, who will tell you what a roaring success her invocation of this clause for the 2017 general election was, with specific reference to 'strong and stable', malfunctioning Maybots, and how to lose a 20-point lead in the polls.

clearly stated: 'This is your decision. The government will implement what you decide.' To which Remainers pointed out that most political promises aren't worth the paper they're written on. To which Leavers cited the exception that proves the rule. And so on. It would be the first, though emphatically not the last, of Brexit arguments so perfectly circular you could make wheels out of them.

Then there was the question of language. No, not the kind of language used by Noel Gallagher at the start of this section: the language used for the question itself. The 1975 referendum question was 'do you think that the United Kingdom should stay in the European Community (the Common Market)?' with a choice of two answers, YES or NO.

The initially proposed question for 2016 was very similar: 'should the United Kingdom remain a member of the European Union?' (Again with a simple YES/NO answer.) But the Electoral Commission feared that the question was, even subconsciously, a biased one. 'It only sets out the "remain" option in the question, and the "yes" response is for the status quo,' the Commission said.

The question was therefore changed to 'should the United Kingdom remain a member of the European Union or leave the European Union?', and it was this one which was put to the electorate in the referendum.

Just a matter of linguistic semantics? Maybe. But Steve Baker, a pro-Leave MP who campaigned for the question to be changed, said that the difference in responses from the first question to the second (that is, the same polling sample asked for their answers to both questions in turn) was 4% – almost exactly the eventual margin of Leave's victory. On such margins might history swing.[8]

'Should the United Kingdom remain a member of the European Union or leave the European Union?' There were two aspects to this question which would become crucial not so much during the referendum as after it.

The first was the use of the phrase 'United Kingdom' – i.e. the UK as a whole, rather than its constituent home nations and/or Gibraltar. The entire union would leave or the entire union would stay, no matter how each region voted.

The second was the simple concept of leaving the EU. How this would be accomplished was not specified: nor was the nature of any future relationship between the UK and the EU.

It was a text whose very simplicity would lead to it being freighted with all kinds of meaning, depending on each individual's interpretation of it.[9]

---

8   You the bluffer will not just know all this: you will go one step further, to the linguistic path not taken. You can point out that 'Remain' was a poor word, and that 'Stay' might have been better. 'Remain' sounds soft, and is associated with leftovers: 'stay' sounds punchier and is associated with steadfastness. Maybe you could broaden the discussion to encompass the possibilities of asking the question in iambic pentameter, haiku or hip-hop rhyme.

9   In this respect, it's a little like the Second Amendment of the US Constitution, which (depending on your viewpoint) allows John Q. Public to arm himself like Arnie in *Commando*, or refers to organised militias from an era when the most powerful weapons available were muskets. (Neither of these interpretations are to be confused with the right to bare arms, which is inadvisable in very cold countries and frowned upon in parts of the Middle East.)

THE ISSUES

The simplicity of the referendum question disguised the multiplicity of issues which voters felt important during the referendum campaign. Some of these issues were localised by region or sector (for example, Northern Ireland and the scientific community respectively had specific concerns about Brexit), but in general the three issues which voters described as most important in their decision on whether to vote 'Remain' or 'Leave' were the economic impact on the UK, the effect on immigration, and the question of national sovereignty.

'Talk about Europe and they call you extreme. Talk about tax and they call you greedy. Talk about crime and they call you reactionary. Talk about immigration and they call you racist; talk about your nation and they call you Little Englanders.'

William Hague, 2001.

- ***The economic impact***. By definition, the economic impact of any decision to leave was, and remains, unknowable. At the time of writing we have not left the EU yet, and once we do it will take several years for the economic impact, positive or

29

negative, to be felt. Even then, it will probably be impossible to quantify it exactly, as (a) so many other circumstances influence any given economic situation, and (b) there will be no way of knowing what the comparative effect of a 'Remain' vote would have been. What we *do* know is that most experts said at the time, and continue to say, that the economic impact of Brexit will be negative. The Chancellor George Osborne and the Governor of the Bank of England Mark Carney were among many establishment figures who warned that a 'Leave' vote would have negative consequences. In response, the Leave campaign argued that less red tape would create more jobs, the freedom for Britain to make its own trade deals would have a positive effect, and that Mystic Meg had a better forecasting record than the Bank of England. (Bluffers can concede that the last bit might have been slightly paraphrased.)

- *Immigration*. A month before the referendum, the Office for National Statistics announced that 630,000 people moved to the UK in 2015, 270,000 of them from other EU member states. (Net migration in 2015, including those who had emigrated, was 333,000.) For the Leave campaign and millions who felt that immigration was too high, this figure was confirmation that they were right (though of course leaving the EU will in itself have no effect on immigration from non-EU countries). And, despite much talk of 'uncontrolled' movement within the EU, even EU citizens can (a) be denied entry to another member state if deemed a security threat, and (b) deported after six months if they have neither a job nor a realistic prospect of one. Remain campaigners said that immigration helped increase both economic output and tax revenue.

- *National sovereignty*. One of the Leave campaign's slogans was 'take back control', which both reflected and fed the widespread belief that Britain had surrendered too much power to Brussels. Under the European Communities Act 1972, EU law is given primacy in the UK, though this statute could always have been repealed by the UK Parliament (as in fact it will be when the UK leaves the EU – see 'legalities' on page 75.) The Remain campaign contended that much EU law is akin to UK law, particularly in areas of commercial legislation, employment and so on, and that the UK has always retained the ability to make its own decisions on vital issues such as defence, taxation, elections and so on.

THE CAMPAIGN

The majority of David Cameron's Cabinet, including the holders of all four 'great offices of state' – Cameron himself, Chancellor George Osborne, Home Secretary Theresa May and Foreign Secretary Philip Hammond – declared themselves for 'Remain', though six ministers, including Justice Secretary Michael Gove, backed 'Leave'. The biggest individual prize for either side, however, was London mayor Boris Johnson, the most charismatic and controversial of all senior politicians.

Johnson eventually declared himself for 'Leave', though the extent to which this was motivated by ideological conviction rather than personal ambition remains unclear. He announced his decision in his weekly *Daily Telegraph* column, having written two drafts of it, one backing 'Remain' and the other 'Leave'. Several friends and colleagues were surprised by the direction in which he jumped. 'I know – because Boris told me, as he told many people – that he's not an Outer,' said Tory MP Sir Nicholas Soames. 'I don't believe his heart is really in it.'

Sir Humphrey: Bernard, if the right people don't have power, do you know what happens? The wrong people get it: politicians, councillors, ordinary voters!
Bernard: But aren't they supposed to, in a democracy?
Sir Humphrey: This is a British democracy, Bernard!

- Yes, Minister

Ironically, or perhaps appropriately, it was Johnson who had long before been responsible for some of the negative public views of the EU. As Brussels correspondent of the *Daily Telegraph* between 1989 and 1994, he had lampooned the European institutions, writing stories about plans to standardise condom sizes, ban prawn cocktail flavour crisps and make bananas straight.

Many of these stories were, at best, exaggerations: when he left Brussels, a colleague at his leaving party declaimed a parody of Hilaire Belloc's *Matilda*: 'Boris told such dreadful lies/It made one gasp and stretch one's eyes.' But the stories were fun and readable, particularly given the turgid nature of most Brussels reporting. And the image which these stories both played up to and reinforced – a monolithic unaccountable Death Star of scheming Eurocrats – found great popularity, not least on the Conservative backbenches of the time. 'I was sort of chucking these rocks over the garden wall and I listened to this amazing crash from the greenhouse next door over in England as everything I wrote from Brussels was having this amazing, explosive effect on the Tory Party – and it really gave me this, I suppose, rather weird sense of power,' Johnson said on *Desert Island Discs* in 2005.

Johnson's decision to back 'Leave' was arguably every bit as important to the cause as the rewording of the referendum question had been. He was, Farage apart, the only genuine populist on either side,[10] a man so famous (or infamous) that he was known simply as 'Boris'. He pulled crowds and drew reporters. He would provide, if nothing else, light relief.

---

10   Jeremy Corbyn is also undeniably a populist, though his ability to galvanise neutral crowds rather than just the party faithful only really came to the fore during the 2017 general election. In fact, he was more or less invisible during the referendum campaign, despite nominally being for Remain: something which led to bitter recriminations from Conservative members of the Remain campaign, who felt that Corbyn could have helped swing it back for them if he'd been more visible and trenchant in his defence of the EU.

And God knows it was needed. The referendum campaign was, let's be honest, pretty underwhelming, no matter who you supported. It wasn't much of a dialogue, as that would have involved each side listening to the other rather than just trying to shout them down or doing the political equivalent of sticking your fingers in your ears and going 'la la la I can't hear you'. Maybe the rise of social media, where people seem keener to insult each other than they do in the real world, had something to do with this: maybe this is just the state of political discourse nowadays. Either way, you could find more civilised debate in a primary school playground.[11]

Both campaigns were short on facts, making claims which were at best questionable and at worst demonstrably false.

False claims: Remain

'[If we leave] we will need an emergency Budget to restore stability to public finances' – George Osborne.

No 'emergency Budget' (which would presumably have been packed with tax rises and spending cuts) took place. Granted, Osborne himself was sacked a month after the referendum, but (a) if a budget was that urgent, he could have issued one in the time available, and (b) his successor Philip Hammond, who is like Osborne both a Tory and a Remainer, didn't issue one either.

---

11 Is it too much to ask that next time there's a national plebiscite it's announced outside a kebab shop in the small hours of Sunday and held the following week, on a Thursday as per? Five days would seem about the optimum length of time for a campaign. This one felt like five millennia.

'Two-thirds of British jobs in manufacturing are dependent on demand from Europe' – Alan Johnson.

The actual figure is around 17%. The 'two-thirds' claim was based on comparing the total number of manufacturing jobs (2.55m) with the 1.7m jobs *in all sectors* which the Centre of Economics and Business Research (CEBR) classified as dependent both directly and indirectly on EU trade. Apples and oranges, Alan me old china.[12]

False claims: Leave

'Once we have settled our accounts, we will take back control of roughly £350m per week' – Boris Johnson.

This was derided by the UK Statistics Authority as 'a clear misuse of official statistics'. £350m is the gross UK contribution to the EU, but doesn't take into account (a) money invested in the UK as part of EU projects and (b) the rebate which the UK receives. These between them take the figure down to £250m – an annual difference of £5.2bn.[13]

Turkey (population 76 million) is joining the EU' – Vote Leave publicity.

Turkey has long been a candidate for EU membership, but (a) it has adopted only one of the

---

12 To be fair, Johnson – a genial former postman who left school with no qualifications – has always admitted to his lack of expertise in this context. When appointed shadow chancellor in 2010 he famously quipped that his first act would be to 'pick up a primer – economics for beginners.' He resigned less than four months later.

13 Johnson – or rather this Johnson, Boris, as opposed to Alan – has admitted that the £350m figure was wrong. 'There was an error on the side of the bus,' he told *The Guardian* in January 2018. 'We grossly underestimated the sum over which we would be able to take back control.' He said that the UK's weekly contribution would rise to £438m by the end of a post-Brexit transition period.

35 sets of legal fields (known as chapters) which are necessary for membership and (b) several existing members, including Germany, have indicated that they would use their veto to block Turkish accession. Turkish membership of the EU is akin to QPR's chances of winning the FA Cup: not technically impossible, but equally not remotely plausible in this world or any conceivable parallel one.

Both sides were also long on rancour, appealing in different ways as much to fear as to hope. The Remain campaign even made a virtue of this with their so-called 'Project Fear', concentrating on the manifold disasters which would surely befall Britain if it voted to leave and rarely mentioning the more positive aspects of the EU – maintaining peace and unity on the continent, creating the largest single market and economic unit in the world, enabling citizens to work and live across more than two dozen countries, helping spread western economic thinking to the former communist states of central and eastern Europe, and so on.

The Leave campaign went big on fears of EU expansionism and – particularly in the case of the unofficial Leave.EU group to which Farage had attached his colours – of immigration. This culminated in Farage's unveiling of the 'BREAKING POINT' poster showing a line of immigrants at the Slovenian border – a poster which many saw as resembling Nazi propaganda photographs, and which saw Farage reported to the police for inciting racial hatred.

The poster was unveiled on the same day as the

campaign's one note of genuine tragedy, the murder of pro-Remain MP Jo Cox. The previous day, Farage had been involved in a moment of farce when, leading a flotilla of anti-EU fishermen up the Thames, he had exchanged insults with Remainer Sir Bob Geldof. Farage's choice of a naval blazer bore an uncanny resemblance to the dress sense of Alan Partridge during the shooting of his commercial for Hamilton's Waterbreaks.[14]

The main difference between the two campaigns, and probably the factor which turned the result more than any other, was the respective aims of their appeals. Given that Greece's travails have been instrumental in damaging the image of the eurozone as an unqualified success, you the bluffer should reference Aristotle here.[15]

In his *Rhetoric*, he wrote of three main modes of persuasion: *logos*, *pathos* and *ethos*. The Remain campaign concentrated on the first, using facts and figures to try and persuade voters through logic and an appeal to reason that they were better off inside the EU rather than outside. These arguments may have been factually correct (some of them, anyway), but they were also, for lack of a better word, boring. They promised no excitement of

---

14 Needless to say, Partridge himself is a staunch Brexiteer, describing it as a political hot potato 'up there with the NHS, North Korea and the cycle lane epidemic', and saying he knows 'how liberating it can feel when a loved one leaves after staying with you for a prolonged period. And that's how I and millions of others feel about the EU. We've enjoyed having Brussels kip in the spare room, sharing some Christmas cheer. But we want the spare room back (for storage or whatever), and have had enough of asking what Poland wants for dinner, or if Greece minds turning the TV down because the volume is absolutely ridiculous.'

15 If you're feeling extra-confident, then you can even mention Plato and Socrates too, but make sure you mean the Greek blokes rather than the Touring Car champion/TV presenter and the former Brazilian football captain respectively.

shaking up the system, which was in any case a status quo which hardly encouraged unconditional love. Relatively few people in the UK, even among the many who voted Remain, feel great emotional attachment to the EU.

But many more feel such attachment to their country. So the Leave campaign concentrated on *pathos*, appealing to people's emotions – their feelings that British sovereignty was being eroded, that the country's values were not the same as those of a federal Europe, that 'take back control' referred not just to people's countries but their own lives too. Leave used images of wartime heroism, referring to a 'battle for Britain' and 'Independence Day'. And Leave certainly used social media, which deals far more in emotion than in logic, much better than Remain did.

In doing so, Leave both bolstered and reflected Aristotle's theory of *ethos*: that much of any argument depends on the speaker. In Johnson and Farage – or, as they were styled, Boris and Nigel – Leave had the two most recognisable politicians, both of whom had made their names through cocking a snook at authority and claiming to represent the common man. Johnson with his eccentric humour, Farage with his 'pie-and-a-pint' image: for millions of voters, these men were more credible representatives than David Cameron and George Osborne, widely seen as out-of-touch metropolitan elitists whose private schooling and Oxford education had left them incapable of understanding the hopes and fears of ordinary people.[16]

For millions of people, increasing globalisation and four

---

16 Boris Johnson had been at Eton and Oxford too, of course, but among his many political qualities was his ability to downplay this. And lest it be forgotten, Nigel Farage is also an ex-public schoolboy – in his case, Dulwich College.

decades inside the EU had meant no real improvement to their lives – quite the opposite. Working conditions were precarious, wages were stagnant, living costs and inequality were rising. Whether or not EU membership was responsible for this, and whether or not leaving the EU would improve things, couldn't be known: but if the status quo wasn't working for you, why not vote to change it? Or, as pertinently, why vote not to change it?

For many people, disillusioned with successive governments of whatever hue, this promised to be the only chance they had to make a difference: the only time when neither the Bonzo Dog Band ('no matter who you vote for, the government always gets in) nor P. J. O'Rourke ('if voting changed anything, they'd abolish it') would be proved right.

TWO TRIBES

Inevitably, celebrities were drafted in to express their own preferences.

'When two tribes go to war
A point is all that you can score.'

'Two Tribes', Frankie Goes To Hollywood.

In the blue corner, for Remain, were Keira Knightley, Benedict Cumberbatch, David Beckham, Rio Ferdinand and John Barnes. In the red corner, for Leave, were Sir Michael Caine, John Cleese, Liz Hurley, Sol Campbell and Ian Botham. Looking at that line-up, you'd fancy Team

Remain's chances in a five-a-side, but you'd probably rather have a night out on the piss with Team Leave.

And teams, or tribes, is exactly what supporters of each side were becoming. This is Brexit's most obvious immediate legacy. A general election, even a vicious one, involves several different issues and several different parties, some of whose MPs can just about collectively fit in a phone box (here's looking at you, Lib Dems).[17]

But the referendum was binary: remain or leave, in or out.

There were cautionary voices. A month before polling date, Max Hastings wrote in the *Daily Mail* that 'we are not being offered a choice between good and evil, Satan's emissaries and the angels. We shall be asked to make a marginal judgment call, which is what most of grown-up life is about.'

But such nuance was becoming increasingly hard to find. Positions were becoming more entrenched across the country (fuelled by the media taking sides: tabloids largely for Leave, broadsheets largely for Remain, and the BBC being frantically accused of bias by both sides, which probably means they got it just right).

---

17 And that's not to mention the 'fringe' candidates such as Lord Buckethead, would-be conqueror of Theresa May in her Maidenhead constituency in the 2017 general election, whose manifesto included:

'strong, not entirely stable leadership'

the nationalisation of Adele

the blasting into deep space of any child who misbehaves three times

and a referendum on whether or not to have another Brexit referendum.

These are Buckethead's ideas, to be clear, though you could be forgiven for confusing them with actual government policies. And of course, had he beaten the Prime Minister, he'd have had to renounce his peerage in order to take up his seat in the House of Commons.

Anecdotal evidence poured in of friendships and even families sundered by rival stances. 'Remainers' and 'Leavers' became 'Remoaners' and 'Brexshiteers'. The group identity became paramount: if you weren't with one side then you were against them. Two-thirds of people said that their Brexit stance was more important than their party political affiliation. It wasn't just that Brexit caused faultlines: it exposed some faultlines that were already there but had through accident or design been long hidden.

It is a short step from disagreeing with someone on one issue to seeing them as the embodiment of everything you disagree with and disapprove of.

How they see....	*Remainers*	*Leavers*
Remainers	Enlightened, globalist, cultured, outward-looking, liberal, tolerant, progressive.	Racist, ignorant, insular, xenophobic, uneducated, selfish, reactionary, parochial, Little Englander, nostalgic for a non-existent past.
Leavers	Snobbish, metropolitan, out of touch, pretentious, disloyal, unpatriotic, treacherous.	Patriotic, steadfast, staunch, dependable, principled, clear-eyed, sensible, quintessentially British.

Not only was this proving to be the case, but the differences between the two sides were indeed much more wide-ranging than where they put their 'X' on a ballot paper. Polling after the referendum from the British Election Study and YouGov showed that, when compared to Remainers, Leavers are:

1. more likely to consider prison as punishment rather than rehabilitation

2. twice as likely to think that golliwogs are inoffensive

3. twice as likely to think the BBC should be privatised

4. twice as likely to think that schools are well-funded

5. twice as likely to think that fracking is safe

6. twice as likely to think that gay sex is unnatural

7. twice as likely to want to ban the burqa

8. three times as likely to support the death penalty

9. five times as likely to want to withdraw from the Paris climate change agreement

10. ten times as likely to think Donald Trump is a good president.

The simple Remain/Leave dichotomy has been complicated a little since the referendum, with a third group appearing – the 'Re-Leavers'. These are Remain voters who, though standing by their choice, also accept that Brexit is inevitable and should not be hindered or reversed, either by a parliamentary vote and/or a second referendum. Hard Leavers represent 45%, Re-Leavers 23%, Hard Remainers (who still want to try and stop Brexit) 22%, with 9% undecided. This means that more than two-thirds of the electorate want the country to go through with the process of leaving (YouGov's findings do not account for the remaining 1%).[18]

THE RESULTS

'Smile at us, pay us, pass us; but do not quite forget;
For we are the people of England, that never have spoken yet.'

G. K. Chesterton, The Secret People.

17.4m (if you want to be pedantic, which is after all one of the few genuine pleasures left in life, 17,410,742) people voted to leave the European Union. It was the biggest single political mandate in British history, a

18   Re-Leavers are not to be confused with: Relievers, whose bladders are not what they once were; Believers, which is what the Monkees were when they saw her face; or Beliebers, who are fans of pop star Justin Bieber (ask your children). And the waters may have been muddied by Nigel Farage's statement in January 2018 that arch-Remainers 'will go on whinging and whining and moaning all the way through this process. So maybe, just maybe, I'm reaching the point of thinking that we should have a second referendum on EU membership, and we may just finish the whole thing off…the percentage that would vote to leave next time would be very much bigger than it was last time round.'

statistic which is perhaps less impressive than it first seems (referendums – or, to be even more pedantic, referenda – only have two choices where general elections have several, and the British population is higher than it has ever been before). In fact, the second biggest political mandate ever was supplied by the 16.1m people (all right, all right, the 16,141,241) who voted to remain. Leave secured 51.89% of the vote, Remain 48.11%.

Beyond the national figures, regional breakdowns showed where and how the country was divided. England and Wales voted to leave, Scotland and Northern Ireland to remain. Cities in general voted Remain: rural constituencies voted Leave. Seven out of the ten most heavily Remain areas were in London (though Gibraltar, with 96% voting in favour, was the most Remain area of all[19]): nine out of the ten most Leave areas were in the East Midlands and eastern England (including four in Lincolnshire).

Whether or not a 4% majority for the most seismic decision in British politics since 1945 was 'enough' is endlessly debatable, and also totally irrelevant. The rules of the referendum were that a simple majority was enough, and the Leave campaign had easily secured that – 'without a shot being fired', Farage said, appearing to forget the horrific murder of Jo Cox the previous week.

---

19   Which is understandable, given Gibraltar's fear that Spain wants to reconquer the Rock the moment Britain's back is turned: but it's also ironic, given that in many ways Gibraltar is simply a sunnier, hotter version of the British seaside towns which tended to vote Brexit.

Cameron, who had staked his premiership on winning the referendum, could hardly get out of there fast enough, resigning before most people had finished their breakfast in order to spend more time with his directorships.

WINNERS AND LOSERS

Such a bruising campaign inevitably had its fair share of winners and losers, of triumphs and disasters, of success and failure. Once the dust had cleared, it was possible to see who'd ended up where.

Winners
Boris Johnson. His gamble had paid off: as the standard-bearer of the Leave cause, he was more or less guaranteed a top job in government, even if THE top job didn't come his way after a series of plot twists which stunned viewers of the wildly popular *Game Of Thrones* spin-off series *Tory Bloodletting*. During the Conservative leadership campaign, BoJo managed to snatch defeat from the jaws of victory by managing to hack off both Andrea Leadsom and Michael Gove with his dithering. But overall, he was a winner: Theresa May put Britain's least diplomatic man in charge of the diplomatic service. Who says she has no sense of humour?

Nigel Farage. For forcing the referendum in the first place, for giving himself a media profile which will remain high for years to come – surely at least one of *Strictly Come Dancing, I'm A Celebrity* or a seat in the

Lords beckons? Now bezzies with Donald Trump too, who credited Brexit with helping show that aggressive underdog campaigns (such as, of course, his own presidential run in 2016) can work.

Andrea Leadsom. Few people outside Westminster had heard of her before Brexit, yet as an ardent Leaver she showed well enough in the Tory leadership campaign to secure herself a place in the Cabinet. She reached a run-off with Theresa May before rendering her own chances moot by appearing to suggest that May's lack of children might impinge on her ability to be Prime Minister.

Losers
David Cameron. Obviously. Staked his premiership on the result and fell on his sword the moment it became apparent the gamble had failed. Even then, he was widely criticised for not staying on to help sort out the mess he'd caused. Like Tony Blair with Iraq, this is what Cameron will be remembered for, and his failure will overshadow everything else he achieved in government.

George Osborne. Like Cameron, nailed his colours to the Remain mast and was hoist by his own petard. (That's enough pirate analogies – Ed.) Was summarily dismissed not just as Chancellor but from the Cabinet altogether by Theresa May. Got some kind of revenge by becoming editor of the *Evening Standard*, where he tries to ration himself to no more than a dozen anti-May stories a day. Maybe they're just trying to hide their true feelings for each other. Then again, maybe not.

Michael Gove. Ah, Govester. You survived the rigours of the campaign. You survived your wife Sarah Vine turning all Lady Macbeth in the *Daily Mail* after the referendum when she wrote that 'given Michael's high-profile role in the Leave campaign, he – we – are now charged with implementing the instructions of 17 million people.' *We? WE?* You survived the reports that your friendship with David Cameron had been sunk below the waterline by your decision to go against him. And then you laid your knife against the whetstone, made it as sharp as you possibly could, and stabbed Boris Johnson – the man for whom you had been campaign manager – in his broad blond back, and the Wrath of the Tory Faithful was great indeed.

ℬ

'I'll go for a pint of something and think to myself that, after 25 years of slog, perhaps it was all worth it.'

Nigel Farage, on the triggering of Article 50,
29 March 2017.

ARTICLE 50

Now and then, a minor point of procedure hitherto unknown by anyone other than the most wonky of political wonks becomes not just common knowledge, but also the topic of frenzied discussion among myriads of instant experts.

It happened in November 2000, when the destiny of the US Presidential election appeared to depend on hanging chads.[20]

It happened in 2010, when the failure of any party to gain an overall majority in the general election led to much sagacious chin-stroking about 'confidence and supply' arrangements before the Tories and Lib Dems formed a full coalition.

And it happened again in 2016, when suddenly all and sundry could give you chapter and verse on Article 50 (not to be confused with Area 51, Studio 54 or Heinz 57).

---

20 'Hanging Chads' are incompletely punched holes in voting cards rather than the latest hot indie band. Second memo to self: copyright the name for next hot indie band. Third memo to self: form said band.

The bluffer can drop in some oh-I-just-happen-to-know-this-stuff knowledge about some of the other articles in the EU constitution. This is, of course, totally irrelevant to Brexit, but very relevant to making it look as though you know your EU onions.

- Article 2 states the founding values of the EU, which are quite important but unfortunately sound more or less like the usual guff about respect for freedom, democracy, equality, tolerance and so on – that is, the kind of stuff wearingly familiar to anyone who has worked in a company with a 'mission statement' and/or bought a Hallmark card.
- Article 5 sets the principles of conferral, subsidiarity and proportionality: catnip to the bluffer, who can wax lyrical about these safe in the knowledge that almost no-one will be able to call his bluff.
- Article 22 gives the European Council, acting unanimously, control over defining the EU's foreign policy.
- and Article 49 deals with applications to join the EU.

The text of Article 50 reads:

'Any Member State may decide to withdraw from the Union in accordance with its own constitutional requirements. A Member State which decides to withdraw shall notify the European Council of its intention. In the light of the guidelines provided by the European Council, the Union shall negotiate and conclude an agreement with that State,

setting out the arrangements for its withdrawal, taking account of the framework for its future relationship with the Union. That agreement shall be negotiated in accordance with Article 218(3) of the Treaty on the Functioning of the European Union. It shall be concluded on behalf of the Union by the Council, acting by a qualified majority, after obtaining the consent of the European Parliament. The Treaties shall cease to apply to the State in question from the date of entry into force of the withdrawal agreement or, failing that, two years after the notification referred to in paragraph 2, unless the European Council, in agreement with the Member State concerned, unanimously decides to extend this period.'

The UK invoked Article 50 on 29 March 2017, when Sir Tim Barrow, the Permanent Representative of the United Kingdom to the European Union, formally delivered by hand a letter signed by Prime Minister Theresa May to Donald Tusk, the President of the European Council in Brussels.[21] The two-year time period specified in Article 50 means that the UK will cease to be a member of the EU on 30 March 2019, unless an extension period is agreed by both sides (which it almost certainly will be (see 'Transition' on page 107.))[22]

---

21 Presumably they thought either that an e-mail might end up in Tusk's spam folder, or else they just liked the old-school courtesy of delivering a letter, though clearly Barrow refused to dress either in a butler's morning coat replete with silver salver or in year-round postie shorts while inching gingerly around a barking dog.

22 Think of the extension period as extra time and the two years as the standard 90 minutes of a football match, though almost certainly a tedious 0-0 rather than an end-to-end thriller with the EU equalising late in stoppage time.

Hacker: I've got to make a speech. It's to be to a hostile audience of posturing, self-righteous, theatrical drunks.
Sir Humphrey: *The House of Commons, you mean?*

Yes, Prime Minister

The two main questions concerning Article 50 are (a) did its invocation need parliamentary approval and (b) is it reversible? Clearly, Remainers were in general keener on the answers to both these being 'yes'.

The first question concerning parliamentary approval has already been answered following a Supreme Court ruling in January 2017, which declared that the UK's own 'constitutional requirements' as outlined in the first sentence of Article 50 *did* include the need for parliamentary approval. The government had argued that the royal prerogative, which among other things allows the government to conduct international affairs on the monarch's behalf without parliamentary consent, applied in the case of Article 50.

The counter-argument (in a case actually brought by a private citizen, Gina Miller), was that sovereignty in Britain resides effectively with parliament. Parliament makes (and repeals) laws (the primacy of EU law was one of the reasons many people were disquieted with continued EU membership), and since exiting the EU will involve the most enormous legal retrenchment, this was clearly a matter for Parliament.

The Supreme Court said 'the most fundamental rule of UK constitutional law is that the Crown in Parliament[23] is sovereign and that legislation enacted by the Crown with the consent of both Houses of Parliament is supreme.' (Hence also the royal prerogative over international affairs, because in general these have little or no effect on domestic law and therefore on parliamentary legislation/sovereignty.)

The second question, about Article 50 being reversible, is a harder one to answer: indeed, there is still no consensus on this. Is the UK on a train or a rollercoaster? That is, can the country get off at the next stop and return home (given the usual caveats about signal failures/leaves on the line/the wrong kind of snow), or is it stuck on a given course until the ride comes to an end?[24]

The government has already conceded that Parliament will get a vote on whether or not to accept any final deal with the EU. David Davis told the Commons in November 2017 that 'we need to take further steps

---

23 The concept of the 'crown in parliament' is that of a fusion of executive (government) and legislative (parliamentary) powers: i.e. that the monarch enacts laws on the advice of parliament. It is also often asserted that the UK does not have a constitution. This is untrue, and the bluffer will take great pleasure in pointing this out. The UK has no specific integrated constitutional document, true, but it has plenty of laws and principles which taken together form a constitution in the generally accepted meaning of the word. The extra-confident bluffer can add that these laws and principles come mainly from four sources: statute law (laws passed by the legislature), common law (laws established through court judgements), parliamentary conventions, and works of authority (books by experts on constitutional issues).

24 Perhaps even crashing hard into the buffers at the end if management has decided to delegate health and safety to that spotty kid on work experience.

to provide clarity and certainty both in the negotiations and at home regarding the implementation of any agreement into United Kingdom law. This agreement will only hold if parliament approves it.'

This is in effect the middle course between ardent Brexiteers, who would like the government to push through the best agreement it can without needing parliamentary approval, and ardent Remainers who would like that final deal to be put to the people in another referendum. It is also, of course, a further reflection of parliamentary sovereignty.

As ever with Brexit, however, things are not as simple as they may initially seem. For a start, there is not just one deal – the withdrawal agreement – on the table, but two: there also needs to be an agreement, even in outline, on the future relationship between the UK and the EU. At the time of writing, the government wants both deals to be packaged up into one vote, meaning that parliament must either accept both or reject both: they cannot accept one and reject the other.

Whether this remains the case is not yet clear, and nor is it clear whether parliament will get to vote on any situation in which the government declares 'no deal' – i.e. that they have been unable to reach agreement with the EU on terms for the withdrawal agreement, the new relationship, or both. It may be that the government has to go back to Brussels and say 'yes, we asked parliament to say yes to a no deal but they said no to a no deal but yes to us coming back and asking if you would now say no to a no deal yourselves and yes to a new deal yeah but no but yeah…' (If you think all this sounds Kafkaesque, just wait till you get to the section in 'Brexicon' about the various European councils.)

And what if Parliament reject any deal anyway? Or what if other circumstances before then mitigate against successful negotiations? The man who helped draft the article, Lord Kerr, is one of those who maintains that it is reversible.

'At any stage we can change our minds if we want to, and if we did we know that our partners would actually be very pleased indeed. As far as the treaty is concerned, there are lots of options... [including] the ability at any stage to take back the letter that the Prime Minister sent to President Tusk on 29th March. I'm not a politician. I'm just the guy who wrote the treaty telling you what the treaty means. It is open to us to argue that the terms as they emerge are not quite the ones that we were led to expect: that the costs of coming out are rather different from what it said on the side of the battlebus; that the complexity of coming out was not entirely explained and the effects of coming out on, for example, the NHS or jobs, these things are not what the electorate knew about at the time. If new facts emerge one is entitled to change one's view, as Keynes said. I'm not arguing for a second referendum, I'm saying if we wanted to have a second referendum there is nothing in the treaty, or in the attitude of EU partners, that would prevent us taking the time to have one.'

Other legal experts, such as Hugh Mercer QC and US law professor Jens Dammann, agree with him.[25]

---

25 That these men are not household names is exactly the point for the bluffer: mentioning them suggests you've spent hours arguing obscure points with some of the finest legal brains in the land.

The EU Commission has said that Article 50 'cannot be unilaterally reversed', but here the key word is surely 'unilaterally': that is, the EU would have to agree to any reversal. The European Parliament Brexit committee headed by Guy Verhofstadt spells this out more clearly: 'a revocation of notification needs to be subject to conditions set by all EU27 [the other 27 countries in the EU], so that it cannot be used as a procedural device or abused in an attempt to improve on the current terms of the United Kingdom's membership.'

In contrast, the government has repeatedly said that the process cannot be undone. Former Justice Secretary Liz Truss told Andrew Marr that her 'understanding is that it is irrevocable'. Theresa May has repeatedly said that 'Brexit means Brexit' and that the government will not backtrack, describing the triggering of Article 50 as 'an historic moment from which there can be no turning back'.

But, as with the referendum itself, this seems to come down to the difference between the law and politics. The referendum was not legally binding, but the government pledged to enact the result. There may be no legal impediment to reversing Article 50, but there are huge political impediments. It is not so much that the government *cannot* revoke it, but that they *will not* – at least in the current political circumstances, and indeed in almost any vaguely plausible foreseeable ones too.

Then again, this is a world in which, had you in June 2015 put £10 on a three-way political accumulator of Brexit, Jeremy Corbyn becoming Labour leader and Donald Trump becoming President, you would have made £160,000. (If you'd added Leicester City winning the Premiership to that accumulator, and if you could have found a bookie willing to waive the maximum payout rules (and indeed with enough resources to honour the bet), you'd now be worth... £800m!)

Harold Macmillan famously said that a week is a long time in politics. This applies as much to Brexit as it does to any other part of the political landscape. Only the very brave or the very foolish would say without doubt that they know how this is all going to pan out.

ॐ

Hacker: *So who really runs Europe?*
Sir Humphrey: *Another interesting question. Well done, Minister! The European Union is run on an intricate and sophisticated system based on an hierarchical structure of interlocking and overlapping jurisdictions designed to separate the powers whilst reinforcing the authority of the departments, institutions and agencies who collectively and separately control and supervise the diverse activities of the Union and its associated organisations. So Europe is not run by the president of the European Council or the Council of the European Union but by the president of the European Commission, who is akin to prime minister of Europe because he is elected for five years and heads a Cabinet government whereas the president of the Council, on the other hand, is not elected but appointed, and presides over the meetings of the Council, which is not the Cabinet.*

- Yes, Minister (Brexit special)

DRAMATIS PERSONAE

The success or otherwise of Brexit depends in large measure on the men and women 'in the room' – the negotiators on both sides who are hammering out one of the most complex agreements ever seen. The range of skills they need is mind-boggling: forensic attention to even the smallest detail, ability to build rapport with their counterparts, judgement as to when to twist and when to stick, squaring the circle of being both honest and opaque, the patience to chisel away at an issue in the tiniest increments, and having the stamina and resilience to go long into the night again and again and again. Oh – and all this while every twist and turn in the negotiations is seized upon, distorted, and moulded into quasi-truths, and while constantly being second-guessed by journalists, politicians, and the world and his wife on social media.

For Britain, the process of choosing these people was relatively easy. The Prime Minister established a new department, the Department for Exiting the European

Union (DExEU).[26] And, since many civil servants have dealt with the EU during the normal course of British membership, there were plenty of experienced people around.

For the EU, things were – inevitably – more complicated. As Sir Humphrey's explanation so eloquently details, the EU doesn't like to have one institution where half a dozen will do. In the case of Brexit negotiations, there was a turf war – fought with impeccable politeness and in smart suits, naturally – between the European Commission, the European Council and the European Parliament as to who would lead the talks. Michel Barnier (Commission), Didier Seeuws (Council) and Guy Verhofstadt (Parliament) were all appointed as the EU's Brexit negotiators. As Sir Humphrey's analysis would suggest, the Commission won out (as it usually does in such situations), which explains why Barnier is now the Brexiteers' *bête noire* (or black beast, for those so anti-EU that they can't even bear to speak French).

So who are these men and women who hold so much of Brexit in their hands? A top three from each side here.

In the red, white and blue corner: Team UK.

David Davis. Secretary of State for Exiting The European Union, or, more colloquially, Brexit Secretary. Brexit big

---

26   Not to be confused with Dexy's Midnight Runners, who famously themselves suffered confusion on *Top Of The Pops* when they sang about American soul legend Jackie Wilson in front of an enormous picture of Scottish darts legend Jocky Wilson.

cheese/*grand fromage*/*grosser kase*/*grote kaas*/*gran queso*/
formaggio grande (also available in other EU languages).
One of the Tory Party's 'big beasts'. A former SAS
reservist who grew up on a south London council estate,
and a right-winger who campaigned for Leave. Ran for
the party leadership in 2005 but lost to David Cameron.
A self-styled champion of civil liberties who in 2008,
while the Tories were in opposition, resigned his seat
in protest at Labour's plans for ID cards and extended
detention without charge. (He won it back easily in a
by-election.)

Said by him:
- 'Nobody has ever pretended that this [the Brexit process] will be easy. I have always said that this negotiation will be tough, complex and, at times, confrontational.'
- 'If a democracy cannot change its mind, it ceases to be a democracy.'

Said about him:
- 'He's the only man I know who can swagger while sitting down.' (Anonymous colleague.)
- 'Thick as mince, lazy as a toad and vain as Narcissus.' (Dominic Cummings, Vote Leave campaign manager.)

Oliver Robbins. Lead official for the UK side. Works
out of the Cabinet Office rather than DExEU following
reported tensions with Davis, and reports more or
less directly to the Prime Minister. Served as Tony

Blair's principal private secretary in his early thirties, and gained a reputation as a skilled mediator in the disputes between Blair's No. 10 and Gordon Brown's Treasury – which, given their frequency, would have at least afforded him plenty of practice. Was also deputy national security advisor to David Cameron.

Said by him:

- not much, at least in public. He's a civil servant, and would therefore be unlikely to publicly concede that the sun rises in the east, that the Pope is Catholic, or that there is widespread ursine defecation in sylvan areas.

Said about him:

- 'He really embodied the essence of the impartial civil service, and he's very popular.' (Dame Tessa Jowell, former Olympics minister.)

Sir Tim Barrow. Britain's ambassador to the EU. The 'eyes and ears' on the ground in Brussels. Former ambassador to first Ukraine and then Russia, therefore used to negotiations so difficult that dealing with the EU will surely be child's play in comparison. His role is now to keep informal channels of communication within the various European bodies open. Has the reputation of a low-key but solid operator. Took over from Sir Ivan Rogers, who had accused the government of 'muddled thinking' over Brexit.

Said by him:

- 'Here you go, Don. Letter from your penpal Theresa.' (Or words to that effect when delivering the Article

50 letter to Donald Tusk.) Like Robbins, discreet to the point of Trappism in public.

Said about him:

• 'I have seen him in Brussels. He knows the corridors, he knows the characters. But actually more importantly I saw him in Moscow where he was incredibly resilient as ambassador there, dealing with Putin in a very testing time in our relationship and Tim had a reputation of being bulletproof out there.' – Tom Fletcher, former ambassador to Lebanon.

In the blue and yellow corner: Team EU.

Jean-Claude Juncker. President of the European Commission, and a former Prime Minister of Luxembourg (a position he held for 18 years, which makes Margaret Thatcher (11) and Tony Blair (10) look like fly-by-nights). Seen by many Britons as the natural successor to Jacques 'Up Yours' Delors,[27] an arch-federalist intent on creating a European superstate. Has been in the firing line after leaked papers revealed the extent to which Luxembourg became a tax haven under his premiership.

---

27 Readers of a certain age will remember UP YOURS DELORS, *The Sun*'s front page headline on 1 November 1990 referring to former European Commission President Jacques Delors' attempts to promote further European integration and a single currency for what was then the EC. In the pantheon of famous *Sun* headlines, it's up there with GOTCHA! (about the sinking of the *Belgrano* during the Falklands War), WILL THE LAST PERSON TO LEAVE BRITAIN PLEASE TURN OUT THE LIGHTS? (about the prospect of Neil Kinnock winning the 1992 general election), and FREDDIE STARR ATE MY HAMSTER (about, er, the comedian Freddie Starr eating someone's hamster, which turned out to be a complete fabrication. 'I have never eaten or even nibbled a live hamster, gerbil, guinea pig, mouse, shrew, vole or any other small mammal,' said Starr, who clearly has a future drafting legal contracts if the comedy career doesn't work out.)

Said by him:

- 'Despite what you may read in the British press, I do not want a United States of Europe. I do not believe that Europe can be constructed against the nation state.'

Said about him:

- 'I was going to say he's a piece of work, but that might not translate too well. Is that all right, if I call you a 'piece of work'?' – George W. Bush.

Michel Barnier. Lead negotiator, former French foreign minister. Like Davis, he comes from outside usual political circles (he did not attend the *Ecole Nationale d'Administration*, France's academy for political high-flyers, and for many years was derided as provincial and nicknamed 'the ski instructor' for his organising of the 1992 Winter Olympics). Widely believed to fancy a crack at the Commission presidency when Juncker's term ends in 2019, and knows that a successful Brexit negotiation would greatly enhance his chances.[28]

Said by him:

- 'I'll say it clearly: there's no spirit of revenge, no punishment, no naivety either.'
- 'Keep calm and negotiate.'

---

28 Successful from an EU point of view, of course, though this may not be as reductively zero sum as it seems. There is no mileage (or perhaps kilometreage) for Barnier hammering the UK to the point of no deal, as that would mean that the entire process had been a waste on both sides. Besides, he has to 'sell' any deal to the European Parliament (and the governments of the other 27 countries in the EU) just as much as Theresa May has to 'sell' that deal to Westminster.

Said about him:

- 'His idea of Europe is a Europe of nations and not a federation. I think that in the forthcoming negotiations he will respect the British nation because he is aware of history and his approach is to respect others.' – MEP Michel Dantin.
- 'Crucially, he's of the project. He's a true believer in the religion of building a united states of Europe and so he's the man they're going to trust.' – Nigel Farage.

Sabine Weyand. Barnier's German deputy. Studied at Cambridge and is known for her fierce intelligence, sense of humour and infectious laughter. The latter two qualities must be conspicuous in the halls of Brussels, which are not exactly known for 24/7 funtime. Has more than two decades' experience in trade relations, half of those at the Commission itself. Tasked with some of the trickiest areas, including the Northern Irish border question. Listed in the top 10 most influential women in Brussels by the website www.politico.eu.

Said by her:

- 'Surely spending New Year's Day at the Cape of Good Hope is an auspicious start to 2018.'

Said about her:

- 'She was no-nonsense and honest – she really knew her stuff. She didn't need to look to her assistants for guidance.' – Cecile Toubeau, sustainable transport campaigner.

ʘ̆

Pvt. Pike: *[Singing] Whistle while you work, Hitler is a twerp. He's half-barmy, so's his army, whistle while you work!*
U-boat Captain: *Your name will also go on the list! What is it?*
Capt. Mainwaring: *Don't tell him, Pike!*

Dad's Army

THE NEGOTIATIONS

The 12 'guiding principles' of British negotiating policy were set out in a White Paper of February 2017, and are discussed more fully in the relevant sections of this book. The cynic would argue that 'no plan survives first contact with the enemy', and clearly neither side (unlike Captain Mainwaring) will be giving away trade secrets before they have to, but it's safe to say that the British negotiators will do their best to reach a settlement which honours most, if not all, of these principles.

1. Providing certainty and clarity, including a 'Great Repeal Bill' to remove the European Communities Act 1972 from the statute book and convert existing EU law into domestic law (see 'Legalities' on page 75).

2. Taking control of the UK statute book and ending the jurisdiction of the Court of Justice of the European Union in the UK (see 'Legalities').

3. Strengthening the Union of all parts of the Kingdom, and remaining fully committed to the

Belfast Agreement and its successors (see 'Northern Ireland' and 'Scotland').

4. Working to deliver a practical solution that allows for the maintenance of the Common Travel Area whilst protecting the integrity of the UK immigration system, and which protects the strong ties with Ireland (see 'Northern Ireland' on page 79).

5. Controlling the number of EU nationals coming to the UK (see 'Immigration' on page 89).

6. Securing the status of EU citizens who are already living in the UK, and that of UK nationals in other Member States (see 'Immigration').

7. Protecting and enhancing existing workers' rights (see 'Immigration').

8. Forging a new partnership with the EU, including a wide reaching free trade agreement, and seeking a mutually beneficial new customs agreement with the EU (see 'Trade & Economics' on page 93).

9. Forging free trade relationships across the world (see 'Trade & Economics').

10. Remaining at the vanguard of science and innovation and seeking continued close collaboration with the UK's European partners (see 'Science & Technology' on page 99).

11. Continuing to work with the EU to preserve European security, to fight terrorism, and to uphold justice across Europe (see 'Security' on page 103).

12. Seeking a phased process of implementation, in which both the UK and the EU institutions and the remaining EU member states prepare for the new arrangements (see 'Transition' on page 107).

The extent and nature of progress in each of these areas will be instrumental in shaping the nature of any eventual agreement. That agreement in turn will reflect the kind of Brexit achieved – hard or soft. Unlike in the case of Goldilocks and the three bears, there is probably no 'just right' solution somewhere between these two poles: the public debate around Brexit is so antagonistic and toxic that any agreement is bound to anger as many people as it pleases. Indeed, steering a strictly middle course between those poles would probably leave everyone dissatisfied: one side would perceive it as not going far enough, the other as going too far.

But there are perhaps four main possible general outcomes: soft, Norway, Canada and hard. The government has ruled out some aspects of each of these, saying that the UK will seek its own bespoke deal, but it may still be that when the negotiating process is over the eventual deal looks more like one of these than seems possible right now.

- *Soft*. The UK stays in the single market and customs union, thereby needing to accept all the EU's rules and regulations (especially on the 'four freedoms') and continuing to pay into the EU budget. The UK would continue to have total access to EU trade, but clearly the Leave campaign's pledges to 'take back control' would not have been fulfilled in several areas (borders, money, laws). Since the government has ruled out this scenario, it would probably only be possible after a seismic change in the political landscape, which in turn would almost certainly involve both a general election and another referendum. Over to Brenda in Bristol for what she thinks about this. 'You're joking? Not another one? Oh for God's sake, I can't honestly... I can't stand this. There's too much politics going on at the moment.'

- *Norway*. Norway is in the single market but not the customs union, which means it has to accept the EU's freedom of movement rules but is also allowed to sign trade deals of its own. An exact replica of this deal is unlikely – freedom of movement was one of the crucial issues in the referendum – so perhaps a more probable outcome is the UK leaving the single market too but aligning its rules and regulations with Brussels as far as practically possible. Under this scenario, the UK might (at least temporarily) join either the European Free Trade Association (EFTA), which currently comprises Norway, Iceland, Liechtenstein and Switzerland, and/or the European Economic Area (EEA), which includes all EU countries plus the

EFTA countries but not Switzerland. Needlessly complex? This is Europe.[29]

- **Canada.** The EU signed a comprehensive trade deal with Canada (though it did take seven years to negotiate and ratify, with final approval delayed by one of Belgium's regional parliaments). A similar deal would reduce or remove most customs duties and tariffs, but again the question of financial services would prove difficult – the Canada agreement does not guarantee Canadian firms an EU financial services 'passport'.[30] Canada does not have to contribute to the EU budget, agree to the four freedoms or abide by European Court of Justice (ECJ) rulings, all of which would be catnip to Leavers. The UK would be able to diverge from EU rules and regulations, and be able to forge new trade deals with other nations. Perhaps the most likely course so far.

- **Hard.** Basically everything short of declaring war on Germany. The endpoint of 'no deal is better than a bad deal'. Britain completely disentangles

---

29 Specifically excluded from any such deal: any member of a-ha, the works of Roald Dahl, Edvard Munch's *The Scream*, and the commentary of Bjørge Lillelien who in 1981, following the Norwegian football team's 2-1 defeat of England, famously proclaimed 'We have beaten England! England, birthplace of giants. Lord Nelson, Lord Beaverbrook, Sir Winston Churchill, Sir Anthony Eden, Clement Attlee, Henry Cooper, Lady Diana – we have beaten them all. Maggie Thatcher, can you hear me? Your boys took a hell of a beating! Your boys took a hell of a beating!'

30 Unlike manufacturers, financial services firms need a 'passport' to allow them to practise across the EU rather than simply in their country of origin. This is because the free movement of services is not yet as advanced and integrated as the free movement of goods.

itself from every aspect of EU membership, even by association. Perhaps no trade deal, with all trade governed by World Trade Organisation (WTO) rules – though these rules do not cover financial services, which are vital to Britain's economy. No special border arrangements. The return of high tariffs. Serious disruption in the short term – perhaps even including a ban on British aircraft flying to some EU destinations, which would make the usual airline disruptions look like some sepia-tinted halcyon golden age by comparison.[31] (Aviation matters are also not covered by WTO rules, so if the UK withdrew from the European Common Aviation Area and/or the EU–US Open Skies Agreement, it would need to have an alternative agreement in place.) Of course the country would establish bilateral deals, and would also be free to pursue its own economic course, probably including some kind of deregulation. A tidal wave of change, which Leavers hope would lead to a promised land and Remainers fear will end up in a wasteland.

---

31 If you're one of the many who complain about Ryanair, you would in such circumstances find them suddenly the most desirable low-cost airline around – as an Irish company, they would be unaffected by bans on British aircraft. Not that CEO Michael O'Leary would point this out, shy and retiring chap that he is.

LEGALITIES

The many thousands of EU-derived laws on the UK's books have been implemented under the terms of the European Communities Act 1972. They have come either from EU directives or EU regulations. Directives, despite their name, are not directly effective (those crazy Europeans with their wacky sense of humour again!) and so Parliament has had to pass its own laws to incorporate them into British statute. Regulations *are* directly effective on each member state without the need for national legislation to implement them.

The effect of EU-derived laws on the UK's legislative output is almost impossible to quantify accurately, not least because (a) UK law is also divided into two forms – Acts of Parliament (statutes) and statutory instruments (which detail how statutes will work), and (b) some laws apply to the UK as a whole, while others are passed by devolved assemblies in Belfast, Cardiff and Edinburgh.

Even when you have a number – roughly 60% of all laws introduced in the UK between 1993 and 2014 implemented some form of EU obligations – that

---

Sir Humphrey: *Well Minister, if you ask me for a straight answer, then I shall say that, as far as we can see, looking at it by and large, taking one thing with another in terms of the average of departments, then in the final analysis it is probably true to say, that at the end of the day, in general terms, you would probably find that, not to put too fine a point on it, there probably wasn't very much in it one way or the other. As far as one can see, at this stage.*

- Yes, Minister

---

doesn't give the whole story. Some EU regulations don't affect the UK at all (such as those governing the production of tobacco and olive oil, for example, as these industries don't exist in the UK) but are still agreed and implemented by all members. Some have far more effect on the UK than others – the EU is far more concerned with, say, employment rights and trade regulation than it is with defence, crime and health. Others are to all intents and purposes exactly the same legislation as the UK would pass on its own. And still more deal with matters so small or routine that most people wouldn't regard them as 'law' in the conventional sense: more as administration.

Whatever the true figure and whatever the true

effect, all these laws will, the day after Brexit, refer to an organisation of which the UK will no longer be part. Rather than expunge them all from the books and start again from scratch, the government has proposed a 'Great Repeal Bill' which will repeal the overarching primary act, the ECA 1972 (thus preventing the UK from adopting any further EU legislation) but maintaining existing laws. These laws can then be altered, repealed or amended by parliament in the usual manner.

℞

'*If English votes drag us out of the EU that would be like Britannia waives the rules. There was a democratic vote. We voted to remain. I tell you that the last thing that the people of Ireland need is an EU border with 27 member states stuck right in the middle of it.*'

Martina Anderson, Sinn Fein MEP

HOME NATIONS

NORTHERN IRELAND

The question of Northern Ireland, and in particular the situation with the border between Northern Ireland and the Republic of Ireland, is one of the biggest conundrums thrown up by Brexit. Northern Ireland and Scotland both voted Remain, and the ramifications of that may be significant in the medium to long term, though in very different ways for Northern Ireland than for Scotland.

Northern Ireland is the only part of the UK which has a land border with the EU – the 310 miles of frontier with the Republic of Ireland. At least 30,000 people cross the border every day for work: there are more than 250 crossing points and no physical border controls. Northern Irish people can choose to have British citizenship, Irish citizenship, or both. These are all stipulations of the 1998 Good Friday peace agreement.

Both the UK and Irish governments are committed to maintaining that agreement, not just because any reintroduction of border controls would mean barriers to trade, but also for fear that it would risk relighting the sectarian tensions which blighted Northern Ireland for the best part of three decades. Even at the best of times, Northern Ireland's devolved power-sharing government can seem fragile. Handled wrong, the border question here would equal very much not the best of times.

The Irish government is, unsurprisingly, siding totally with the EU on this one. It has said that Brexit is a UK policy, 'not an EU policy or an Irish policy', and that Brexit is 'bad for Britain, for Europe and for Ireland'. It agrees with the EU position that 'Ireland's priorities are best advanced from a position of strength as a trusted and respected member of the EU27 team.'

Although Dublin has also pledged to 'maintain our close relationship with Britain, which reflects our unique economic, political, cultural and people-to-people links', when push comes to shove the UK can perhaps expect less help from Ireland here than they would like. Dublin's attitude towards the UK on this issue is more or less 'you broke it, you fix it'.

This leaves everyone trying to square the circle: if you need a hard border between the EU and non-EU countries (something on which the EU insists), but if you won't have a hard border between Northern Ireland (part of a country leaving the EU) and Ireland (emphatically still within the EU), then what do you do?

The situation is further complicated by the Common Travel Area (CTA), which allows British and Irish citizens freedom of movement throughout England, Scotland, Wales, Northern Ireland, the Republic of Ireland, the

Isle of Man and the Channel Islands. The CTA has been in existence since 1952 – i.e. long before either the UK or Ireland were part of the EEC. People and goods cross the border between Ireland and Northern Ireland every day as easily as they do between Dorset and Somerset. And suddenly this internal border is an external border.

The EU has suggested that 'flexible and imaginative solutions will be required'. They can say that again. Various suggestions have been put forward, but none of them are without problems:

- Hiving Northern Ireland off to be part of Ireland. Quite apart from the fact that this issue was exactly what the Troubles were fought over – it would be ironic if Brexit achieved what decades of terrorism failed to – the Democratic Unionist Party (DUP) would never stand for it (they are committed to Northern Ireland being part of the UK). And the DUP have a 'confidence and supply' arrangement with the Conservative Party, whose government depends on their support. In other words, the DUP pretty much have a veto on British policy in this area.
- Making Northern Ireland some kind of 'special area', perhaps by bilateral agreement between London and Dublin. This runs counter to everything the EU stands for. From their point of view, you are either in the EU or you are not, and customs is something decided by the entire EU rather than by individual member states. Grant Northern Ireland special status, and who knows which other regions will start demanding similar. The EU has been

shaken enough by the Brexit vote, and maintaining the union's integrity throughout these negotiations will be among their highest priorities.

* Somehow 'shifting' the border away from the Northern Irish/Republic demarcation line. The two most obvious places would be (a) in the Irish Sea between the Irish island and Great Britain and (b) in the Irish Sea off the south coast of Ireland. But neither of these can work properly. The first essentially presumes that Northern Ireland is no longer a part of the UK, which the DUP (and many others) would flatly reject: the second that Ireland is no longer a part of the EU, which the majority of Irish people would equally flatly reject.[32]

Fundamentally, the whole issue is the 21st-century version of the Schleswig-Holstein question, the conundrum vaguely familiar to history pupils of yore which was summed up by Lord Palmerston thus. 'It's so complicated that only three men in Europe have ever understood it. One was Prince Albert, who's dead. The second was a German professor, who went mad. I'm the third, and I've forgotten it.'[33]

---

32 The question of what Michael Flatley himself would or would not flatly reject is only tangentially relevant here.

33 The bluffer can put this whole issue in its proper long-term historical context by pointing out the ancient geographical/linguistic appellations. Ptolemy, the Greco-Roman polymath, called the island of 'great' Britain 'megale brettania' and the smaller island of Ireland 'micra brettania' (Little Britain, not a Japanese car usually painted light mauve and driven by OAPs at 25 mph on open roads, blithely oblivious to the ever-growing tailbacks behind them). If you wish to suggest to an Irishman that his nation is still a smaller and less important part of Britain, make sure that (a) your escape route is clear and (b) you can run faster than him.

SCOTLAND

When Scotland held its referendum on independence in September 2014, those who wanted it to remain part of the UK significantly outnumbered those who wanted independence: the result was 55%-45% in favour of continuing the union which began in 1707. At the time, of course, the UK was still in the EU, and the Brexit referendum was nothing more than a pledge only to be honoured if the Conservatives won an overall majority in the following year's election – something which seemed unlikely.

'As things stand, Scotland faces the prospect of being taken out of the EU against our will. I regard that as democratically unacceptable.'

Nicola Sturgeon, Scottish First Minister

Fast-forward to 2018. The UK is leaving the EU, a decision against which the Scots voted 62-38% (emphatically the biggest margin either for or against in any of the four Home Nations, and with Remain majorities in every one of their 32 council areas): a substantially greater margin than the result in their own independence referendum. A Brexit map showing how regions of the UK voted makes it look as though Great Britain is home to two separate nations with separate values and separate visions of the future: England/ Wales voting to leave, Scotland to remain.

The Scottish National Party (SNP), who hold the largest number of seats north of the border and the third largest overall, has always argued for a second referendum on Scottish independence if there were a 'significant and material change in the circumstances that prevailed in 2014'. Hard to imagine any change more significant and material than Brexit, apart perhaps from supplies of Loch Lomond running dry.[34]

And since the Brexit referendum was for the entire UK – that is, the entire UK had to stay or the entire UK had to leave – the question fundamentally facing the Scots is this: do you want to be part of the UK and out of the EU, or do you want to be part of the EU and out of the UK? (The latter of course assumes that an independent Scotland would apply for admission into the EU and that the EU would accept them. Had the independence campaign won in 2014, this would have been unlikely. It's much more likely now, which in turn makes the independence case stronger.)

A second Scottish independence referendum may still be some way off: some would argue that it makes sense, for example, for the SNP to wait and see the nature of the final Brexit deal before going back to the people, rather than asking them to vote effectively blind. And of course there's no guarantee that the voters would change their minds in sufficient quantities next time round.

---

34 The single malt, obviously, not the actual loch itself.

But if they did, then Brexit would not only mean the sundering of the UK's membership of the EU: it would mean the sundering of the UK itself. This in turn would have huge ramifications. A possible hard border between England and Scotland, for a start, as Scotland would now represent an external EU border.[35] Alternatively, an independent Scotland may well look at whatever solution was found for the Northern Irish border and work off that.

There would be plenty to sort out between Scotland and the rest of the UK if it went independent, not least currency (would Scotland keep the pound?) and defence (the UK's nuclear arsenal is kept at the naval base in the Scottish port of Faslane, and presumably England would want it back).[36] But then again there is plenty to sort out between the UK and the EU right now.

WALES

Although Wales was one of the UK's regions which benefitted most from EU spending (more than £5bn in structural funds since 2000, and £200m per annum from the Common Agricultural Policy), it also voted Leave. Wales is expected to be one of the regions hardest hit by the withdrawal of EU funding post-Brexit.

---

35 Punsters would surely be hoping that Scotland's First Minister at the time be called Adrian, so they can refer to Adrian's Wall. Indeed, if you're (a) Scottish or (b) called Adrian, it may be time to start thinking about a political career more or less purely for this purpose.

36 If only because they'd be mindful of P. G. Wodehouse's dictum that 'it is never difficult to distinguish between a Scotsman with a grievance and a ray of sunshine', particularly when that Scotsman also has his finger on the nuclear button.

In terms of Wales' political status, however, Brexit poses relatively few issues. Unlike Northern Ireland, Wales has no intractable border issues: unlike Scotland, Wales has no large-scale independence movement. Whisper it quietly, but when it comes to Brexit the Welsh are very like the English.[37]

ENGLAND

Many foreigners think England and Britain are the same thing, an opinion shared by many English people too. A Brexit map of England shows pockets of urban Remain surrounded by vast swathes of rural Leave. (Some generalisation may have been applied here.) England voted to leave by the biggest margin (53.4 per cent) of all the Home Nations, and no doubt there are many English leavers who are inclined to think of the whole process as 'Exit' rather than Brexit.

It isn't.

---

37 Whisper it especially quietly at the Millennium Stadium when the Six Nations comes around again and Wales are playing England there.

B

'Whisper it quietly, but when it comes to Brexit the Welsh are very like the English.'

B

'We will remain an open and tolerant country, and one that recognises the valuable contribution migrants make to our society and welcomes those with the skills and expertise to make our nation better still. But in future we must ensure we can control the number of people coming to the UK from the EU.'

Government White Paper, February 2017.

IMMIGRATION

The effect which Brexit will have on immigration levels remains to be seen. Most obviously, of course, it will have no direct effect on numbers of immigrants from non-EU countries, who account for more than 50% of all immigrants into the UK each year. (In 2015, the last year for which figures were available before the referendum, the non-EU/EU split was 57/43.)

Around 3.2m EU citizens work and live in the UK. Their statuses have yet to be determined. In terms of EU migrants entering the UK post-Brexit, the reductions may be fewer than many Leave campaigners would have wanted. The government has indicated that professional workers in many sectors will be fully or partially exempted from migration control, because they will be needed in sectors such as financial services and IT.

Even semi-skilled and unskilled workers cannot entirely be blocked without risking serious economic consequences: EU citizens account for 98% of seasonal horticultural workers, 15% of those working in the hospitality industry, 10% of licensed lorry drivers and 8% of construction workers. Besides, many employers will tell you, officially or unofficially, that workers from other EU countries are often less likely to turn their noses up at mundane or unpleasant tasks than British workers are.

The government will therefore have to balance calls for strict migration controls with the realities of immigrant contribution to the national economy. And any reformed controls will be worthless unless the Home Office and Border Agency can actually enforce them. Forecasts as to actual figures are by nature estimates, but several academics and policy commentators have suggested that the annual post-Brexit reduction in net migration figures (i.e. subtracting the number of those emigrating from the number of those immigrating) could be as little as 50,000. The current net migration figure is 335,000, so this would represent a reduction of 15% – perhaps not the swingeing slash which the Leave campaign had promised. (Indeed, in the short term the number of EU immigrants may actually rise, as they seek to secure their status before the UK leaves the EU.)

The second, and often overlooked, part of the EU immigrant question is its reverse: what happens to UK citizens living elsewhere in the EU? More than a million Britons live elsewhere in the EU (and 35,000 British citizens emigrate to other EU countries every year). Many of these people are retired – and few, if any, EU economies need retirees as badly as they need workers. Together with changes in residency requirements, tax stipulations and healthcare access, many pensioners may decide to return from their idylls in Provence, Marbella and Tuscany.[38] However, several ways of allowing them to keep their current status (or something approximating to it) are under discussion, including 'associate citizenship', which would allow UK nationals to volunteer individually for EU citizenship.

---

38 For those of them who voted Leave, nothing is more likely to make them reconsider than their first English winter back in Blighty, swapping lavender fields or Mediterranean sunsets for an endless damp greyness which is more depressing than an Ingmar Bergman film set to a Joy Division soundtrack. January may only be 31 days long, but each of those days seems to last three weeks.

'The only honest answer about the long-run [economic] consequences is we don't really know.'

Mervyn King
former Governor of the Bank of England.

TRADE & ECONOMICS

The question of what kind of trade deal the UK will end up making with the EU is crucial to the success or otherwise of Brexit, from both parties' point of view.

But what exactly is a trade deal? What does a deal cover, and what does it omit?

Given that many people are holding up the Canadian trade deal with the EU as the kind of model the UK could emulate, in principle though clearly not exactly identical, a quick look at the outline of that deal will give some clues. You can drop in some of this stuff to conversation, safe in the almost sure knowledge that no-one else in the room will have read a trade deal in their lives (and even if they have then that won't matter, as they will be so boring that you will be asleep and therefore unable to have your bluff called by someone who knows more than you do).

The EU's deal with Canada, called the Comprehensive Economic and Trade Agreement (CETA), has 30 separate chapters. These include not just the obvious points such as the removal of tariffs, provisions for mutual investment, competition policy, regulatory co-operation and mutually-agreed parameters on government subsidies, but also things like:

- voluntary co-operation on technical regulations for testing and certifying products
- measures covering food safety and animal and plant health
- mutual recognition of professional qualifications
- domestic regulation ensuring that licensing and qualification requirements and procedures in both the EU and Canada are publicly available, easily understandable, and reasonable
- telecommunications
- electronic commerce
- government procurement, setting out when EU and Canadian businesses can provide goods and services to each other's public sectors
- social and environmental goals
- transparency
- a system for resolving disputes, including a formal mechanism and mediation.

(Told you it was fun.)

Each of these sections is incredibly detailed and involved months if not years of negotiation, hammering out even the smallest of details. The scale of the task facing EU and UK negotiators in attempting to agree a trade deal of their own is clear. It may be that any such deal is easier to achieve than the Canadian one as the UK is by necessity far more regulatorily aligned with the EU than Canada is: then again, it may also be that such a deal is harder as it comes freighted with the kind of political baggage that the Canadians did not have to deal with.

Under the terms of EU membership, the UK is not allowed to hold trade talks with other countries until Brexit is concluded, though it can do 'preparatory work' for such talks – a semantic distinction which will doubtless be wearily familiar to anyone who sees their ex-spouse with someone new and wonders whether they, er, overlapped in their partner's affections.

(In a similar vein, the EU has tried to exclude the UK from sitting in on current EU trade negotiations on the grounds that the UK will soon be effectively a competitor. Theresa May has rejected this idea, saying that 'while we're members of the European Union, we would expect our obligations but also our rights to be honoured in full.' Besides, she doesn't want to be the one who hears all the others laughing at her even before she's closed the door behind her.)

Top of any UK trade deal wishlist is, of course, an agreement with the USA, the UK's single biggest national market (and even as an EU member state, the UK does more trade outside the EU than within it: 57% of UK exports in 2016 were to non-EU countries).

After that (though clearly such deals will be negotiated concurrently as far as possible rather than consecutively) come Australia and New Zealand (the former could give us back The Ashes, for a start), and then countries such as China, India, Japan, the six nations which comprise the Gulf Co-Operation Council

(Bahrain, Kuwait, Oman, Qatar, Saudi Arabia and the United Arab Emirates), South Korea and Switzerland. The latter two have existing trade agreements with the EU (whereas the USA, China, Japan and India do not), but they are unlikely to replicate the terms of those exactly with the much smaller UK market, and will probably want more concessions from London than they have received from Brussels.

The EU is the second largest economic unit in the world, behind the USA. World Bank and IMF figures for 2016 put US GDP at $18.6 trillion, with EU GDP at $16.4 trillion. (China was third, on $11.2 trillion.) Proponents of the single market argue that its four freedoms have permitted and encouraged far greater economic activity than would have been the case in a simple free trade area. And access to this market requires acceptance of these freedoms. No acceptance, no access. So any free trade deal between the UK and the EU will not and cannot offer the same kind of access to the single market as membership does.

So will Brexit make Britain better or worse off? This is for many people the $64,000 question – actually, probably the $64bn question, or even higher – and, as with most forecasts and particularly one where so much depends on the shape of the final deals, is impossible to answer for sure one way or the other.

Certainly, the bulk of expert opinion is that Britain will be worse off outside the EU in the medium and long term. Even the best trade deal reached with the EU will not give the same kind of access that membership of the single market does, which means that bilateral trade deals signed with other countries will have to offer exceptionally advantageous terms to negate this. The extent of the decline depends not just on who you ask but also the nature of any final deal, but consensus is that Britain will be worse off by between 1 and 10% of income per capita.

The Treasury uses more than 20 independent forecasters, based both in the UK and outside it. An average of these forecasters' predictions shows a 0.6% reduction p/a, and a 3% reduction over the course of five years, from papers published in February 2016 (before the referendum) and November 2017. The Office of Budget Responsibility (OBR) came to similar conclusions. This 3% reduction (at a time when their forecasts for the rest of the EU are much brighter) represents about £60bn, or £2,200 per household, and also suggests a £20bn loss in tax revenue – all this for a period ending in c. 2021, when the transition period will only just be over and Brexit proper will scarcely have begun.

The prognosis varies by sector. The City is the focus of particular attention, with several thousand jobs already earmarked for transfer to Paris or Frankfurt (and the headquarters of the European Banking Authority will also be moving to Paris). Trade deals tend to exclude financial services, which means that this lucrative sector will need special negotiation for a new relationship with the EU once Brexit happens and the freedom of movement of services no longer applies. True, bankers aren't exactly the most popular people in the world,[39] but they produce substantial tax revenue if nothing

39 There's a reason why 'merchant banker' is a term in Cockney rhyming slang, and why the popular collective noun for bankers is a 'wunch'.

else. The automotive industry is vulnerable to a loss of freedom of movement of goods, and the construction industry similarly when it comes to freedom of movement of workers.

But weighed against the gloomy prognosis must be two factors. First, that forecasts are notoriously hard to get right, and indeed usually end up partially or totally wrong. For example, though the referendum has had some negative economic effects, such as a fall in the value of sterling and a rise in inflation, these have not been nearly as bad as both the Bank of England and the most pessimistic and doom-mongering of Remain campaigners were predicting.[40]

Second, by the time Brexit has fully played out, which may not be until midway through the 2020s, it will be very difficult to look at whatever Britain's economic situation is then and disentangle which aspects are due to Brexit and which are due to a myriad of other factors.

---

40 That said, economists such as Jonathan Portes of King's College London say that short-term economic forecasting is more unreliable than long-term forecasting, comparing the two to weather and climate respectively: perhaps a little counter-intuitively, it's easy to get tomorrow's weather wrong, but data models for climate change over decades are much more accurate.

SCIENCE & TECHNOLOGY

'Science has always transcended national borders, and there is a real will on all sides to ensure that Brexit does not hinder that.'

Sir Venki Ramakrishnan,
President of the Royal Society.

Science, technology and innovation have all long been areas in which the UK's membership of the EU has been vital. The UK contributes 12% of the total EU budget but receives 15.5% of its science support, including 22% of all grants from the European Research Council since 2007. As part of Brexit, the UK will also be withdrawing from Euratom, which governs nuclear research. Large scientific projects nowadays are usually multinational: as Stephen Hawking says, 'gone are the days when we could stand on our own, against the world. We need to be part of a larger group of nations'.

So it's small wonder that most scientists dread the consequences of Brexit: more than 50% think Brexit will be 'very harmful', another 25% think it will be 'harmful', and less than 10% see any benefit.

Their fears can be summarised into three main areas: money, people, and respect.

- **money**. The flagship €75bn Horizon 2020 (H2020) programme is widely seen as crucial to science both in the UK and EU. The government has pledged to pay British contributions to H2020 projects after Brexit, provided that bids are submitted before the day of British departure. The UK could still participate in H2020 after Brexit as an 'associated country', though it would no longer get a vote. The status of other less prestigious programmes remains to be seen. The consultancy Digital Science estimates that losing EU research funds would deprive UK scientists of £1bn a year. In addition, much British research relies heavily on imported equipment, which is more expensive with a weak pound (as is membership of non-EU bodies such as CERN and the European Space Agency, whose subscriptions are set in Swiss francs and euros respectively).

- **people**. Around 16% of university researchers, and 23% of academic staff in biology, mathematics and physics alone, are non-UK EU nationals. Many of them may neither have permission nor the inclination to stay after Brexit, especially since some do not earn enough to qualify on 'skilled worker' visa programmes. The University of Cambridge expects EU student intake to collapse by two-thirds after Brexit. Immigration policies are therefore hugely important to the scientific community. 'We need to fight to attract talented scientists and engineers from the global pool, not to reluctantly allow them in,' said Sarah Main, executive director of the Campaign for Science and Engineering (CaSE). Perceptions and reports of increased xenophobia and insularity may also deter EU scientists from wishing to work in the UK.

- *respect*. Britain has long been at the forefront of science, with more Nobel laureates than any country bar the USA and some of the most famous names ever to conduct an experiment, such as Isaac Newton, Charles Darwin, Francis Crick and Tim Berners-Lee. But many scientists feel that the referendum result was more or less two fingers to their way of working and the things they hold dear. Former EU science adviser Dame Anne Glover said 'the referendum had nothing to do with evidence. Scientists made a big mistake because we assumed that providing facts and evidence would be compelling – and we were entirely ignored.'

'National security will be less directly affected by Brexit than many other policy areas. This is because security has always been the responsibility of individual member states, not the EU, as European Union treaties recognise.'

Sir Mark Lyall Grant,
national security adviser 2015–17.

SECURITY

Terrorism, crime and security are high on any government's agenda. Will Brexit make the UK more secure, less secure, or will it have little practical effect?

On one hand, Brexit will – in theory, at least – allow the UK to have greater control of its borders. But this, as in the case of immigration, will be dependent on the extent to which the Home Office and Border Agency have the manpower and resources to carry out their jobs effectively.

And, even as an EU member, Britain has maintained a much higher level of border control than many other EU countries, not just through the simple geographical reality of being an island but also through the country's refusal to join the Schengen area which allows movement without checks.[41] Richard Walton, former

---

41   A look at the perpetrators of or prime suspects for the five terrorist attacks carried out in the UK in 2017 show a mixture of British nationals, non-EU immigrants and those with some EU connection:

British nationals: Khalid Masood, who carried out the Westminster Bridge attack on 22 March; Salman Abedi, the Manchester Arena suicide bomber on 22 May; Kharam Butt, one of the London Bridge attackers on 3 June; Darren Osborne, the Finsbury Park mosque attacker on 19 June.

continued overleaf

Non-EU: an unnamed Iraqi orphan refugee who has been charged with the London tube attack on 15 September.

EU connection: Rachid Redouane, London Bridge attacker, a Moroccan citizen who lived in the UK on an Irish residency card; Youssef Zaghba, London Bridge attacker, dual Moroccan and Italian nationality.

Metropolitan Police Counter-Terrorism Commander, said 'the UK could leave both the EU with little, if any, impact on its own national security or counter-terrorism capabilities.'

On the other hand, leaving the EU may mean disruption in terms of intelligence-sharing and trans-border co-operation with other EU countries. This in turn could lead to vital intelligence being missed about, say, jihadist attacks whose personnel and/or weapons come through the EU en route to the UK.

Europol director-general Rob Wainwright said that the UK's 'law enforcement community has become dependent on the unique operational benefits offered by key EU instruments.' But equally much intelligence work is done by UK agencies either on their own or in bilateral agreements with, for example, their French and German counterparts. These bypass Europol and similar bodies altogether, if only to avoid the bureaucracy and lack of secrecy which come with sharing information with more than two dozen other nations.

In larger military terms, NATO rather than the EU is responsible for the defence of Europe, and the UK is not leaving NATO. The UK is also the only European member of the 'Five Eyes' group, comprising the US, the UK, Canada, Australia and New Zealand. This Anglosphere alliance is more important to British intelligence than the EU has ever been – the five countries share a large amount of sensitive and high-grade intelligence – and this membership will also be unaffected by Brexit.[42] So overall, Brexit will probably have relatively little effect on the UK's security.

---

42 The 'Five Eyes' issue is prime bluffing territory. Should you be so inclined (and as a bluffer you should be so inclined, or else why are you reading this book?), you can casually drop in one or more of the following:

that 'Five Eyes' is often abbreviated to FVEY

that the alliance has since the 1960s co-operated in running a mass surveillance programme named ECHELON, which began as telephone tapping but has since expanded to cover e-mails and the internet

that the names of other FVEY surveillance programmes sound as if they've been taken from a Jason Bourne movie: Prism, Tempora, Muscular, Stateroom. (Well, either a Bourne film or an online fetish chatroom)

that often one of the five nations will spy on the other's citizens, and vice versa, in order to circumvent their own domestic laws. If you're in Northampton, for example, you're probably being eavesdropped by some bloke called Shane in Adelaide who now and then cracks open another cold one and prefaces every sentence with the compound word 'ahyeahlookmate'.

The true bluffer will preface any discussion about FVEY by beckoning their interlocutor into the nearest kitchen/bathroom, turning the taps on, checking for likely locations of hidden cameras to avoid the possibility of lip-reading, and only then dropping some Bluffer Knowledge Bombs. After all, it's not paranoid if they really are after you.

Sir Humphrey: To put it simply, Prime Minister, certain informal discussions took place involving a full and frank exchange of views out of which there arose a series of proposals, which on examination proved to indicate certain promising lines of inquiry, which, when pursued, led to the realisation that the alternative courses of action might, in fact, in certain circumstances, be susceptible of discreet modification, leading to a reappraisal of the original areas of difference and pointing the way to encouraging possibilities of compromise and cooperation, which, if bilaterally implemented with appropriate give and take on both sides might, if the climate were right, have a reasonable probability at the end of the day of leading, rightly or wrongly, to a mutually satisfactory resolution.

Hacker: What the hell are you talking about?

Sir Humphrey: We did a deal.

Yes, Prime Minister

TRANSITION

The UK is due to leave the EU at 11pm UK time (midnight in Brussels) on 29 March, 2017. That's the date set by Theresa May and delivered to Donald Tusk by Sir Tim Barrow. Simple, huh?

Not exactly. It's clear that, even if the UK and EU do reach and ratify the two agreements they need to conclude (the withdrawal agreement and the new relationship) – and that is a big 'if', an 'if' so big you could stick landing lights on it and use it to guide aircraft into Heathrow – there's no way that those agreements will be implemented in time.

Therefore, both sides have in principle agreed to a transition period, which will at the very least allow government departments, businesses and other parties time to prepare themselves for and comply with whatever new regulations have been agreed. This transition period will almost certainly be needed for negotiations as well, in some sectors if not all.

How long will this period be? The UK have suggested two years, taking it to the end of March 2021. The EU have said it can go no further than 31 December 2020, as this coincides with the end of the EU's seven-year budget period. The difference is three months, which may not sound like a lot, but in a transfer of power this complex it's arguable that every day counts.

The EU will almost certainly get its way on this one, as all 27 EU countries have to agree to any extension of the Article 50 process beyond March 2019, and they are far more likely to agree to their own preferred date than to the UK's, especially given the budget period. (The Labour Party support the idea of a transition period, but without specifying the parameters of that period other than being 'as short as possible but as long as necessary'. Really helpful, Jezza.)

But the real question of the transition period is not whether it will happen or how long it will last, but how it would work. The EU has already said that any transition period could 'only happen on the basis of the existing EU regulatory, budgetary, supervisory, judiciary, enforcement instruments and structures'. There seems no way for it to be operational other than this, as a continuation of existing EU rules and regulations – that is, there's no way that one set of circumstances could be negotiated for a transition period and then another for Brexit itself, as there's simply not time for that. Britain would probably stay in the single market and continue to contribute to the EU budget, but it would not have a vote after March 2019.

Call it a 'standstill agreement', call it keeping Britain in the EU in all but name, it all ends up in the same place – that having said Britain will be leaving in March

2019, it won't actually be doing so properly for another 21 months, which means that Britain will be like those ghastly people who put their coats on in the hall as though they're about to leave a party and then spend a further two hours yabbering away to all and sundry.[43]

How much this will cause problems for Theresa May with both discontented Eurosceptic backbenchers and public opinion on the Leave side remains to be seen. It will at the very least involve some legal legerdemain, as the Great Repeal Bill which will strike the 1972 European Communities Act from the statute book will need to be either held in abeyance or counteracted by another piece of legislation allowing the UK to continue under EU law until the end of transition. This will also mean that the UK will remain under the auspices of the European Court of Justice, which is among Brexiteers' biggest *bêtes noires*.

---

43 The kind of people, in other words, who treat The Clash's famous question 'Should I Stay Or Should I Go?' as a philosophical conundrum on a par with that of Schrödinger's Cat (see *The Bluffer's Guide to the Quantum Universe*.) They are the guests who are simultaneously attending the party and not attending it, who have at the same time left and not left.

There's no point in pretending that you know everything about Brexit – nobody does – but if you've got this far and you've absorbed at least a modicum of the information and advice contained within these pages, then you will almost certainly know more than 99% of the rest of the human race about what it involves, how it might be good for the UK, how it might be bad for the UK, why the issues are often misunderstood, and why Brexit dominates and will continue to dominate the political landscape for the foreseeable future.

What you now do with this information is up to you, but here's a suggestion: be confident about your new-found knowledge, see how far it takes you, but above all have fun using it. You are now a bona fide expert in the art of bluffing about the greatest schism in the country since 1651.

BREXICON: A BREXIT GLOSSARY

A few technical terms can be putty in the hands of the skilled bluffer. Pepper your conversation with references to some of these, and people will think you know more about Brexit than David Davis and Michel Barnier put together.[44]

Acquis communautaire: the entire body of EU rights and obligations – i.e. treaties, EU legislation, case law of the Court of Justice of the EU, declarations and resolutions, instruments under the Common Foreign and Security Policy, international agreements and so on. The combination of high legal concept and French makes *acquis communautaire* a potent bluffer's weapon, especially if you just drop a casual 'acquis' here and there, as though the abbreviation's no big deal. Wield it wisely.

---

44 Probably not that difficult, come to think of it.

Article 50: the relevant section of the European Union (EU) Treaty, inserted into that document by the 2009 Lisbon Treaty, which both allows a member state to leave the EU and sets out procedures and timescales for doing so.

Brexit: abbreviation for 'British exit' from the EU. May originally have stemmed from 'Grexit', the possibility of Greece leaving the EU during its own economic crisis. Now universally used to cover not just the procedure of leaving but pretty much everything around the many issues too. Due to happen at 11pm on 29 March 2019, though will be subject to a transition period after that.

Brexit means Brexit: according to Theresa May, somewhere between stating the bleeding obvious and channelling her inner Yoda.

Charter of Fundamental Rights of the European Union: first proclaimed in 2000, and given legally binding status nine years later under the Lisbon Treaty, these are a set of basic political, social, and economic rights for EU citizens and residents divided into six categories: Dignity, Freedoms, Equality, Solidarity, Citizens' Rights, and Justice.

Cliff edge: a geographical feature over which the UK will go if it leaves the EU, the single market and the customs union without a trade deal lined up. Exports would be subject to tariffs, goods no longer accredited for sale in the EU, planes unable to fly to or from EU airports, customs checks and administrative chaos. This particular cliff edge is therefore located just above Shit Creek, a locale where the paddle shop is firmly closed.

Common Agricultural Policy (CAP): one of the cornerstones of the EU's list of competences (qv). Established in 1962 under the EEC, and aimed at supporting food production, managing natural resources and developing rural areas. In the minds of many British who can remember that far back, associated in no particular order with butter mountains, wine lakes, and the French treating the CAP as their own fiefdom.

Common Commercial Policy: allows the EU to negotiate on behalf of its member states over imports (goods, services, intellectual property rights etc.)

Common Travel Area: an open borders area comprising the UK (including the Channel Islands and the Isle of Man) and the Republic of Ireland. Some form of this has existed since the Irish Free State was created in 1922. Allows UK and Irish citizens to cross internal borders with minimal identity documents.[45]

Competence: the granting of power to a body in a particular policy area. The EU treaties confer certain competences on the EU and some or all of its constituent

---

45   These may or may not include a driving licence, a student railcard, a Blockbuster membership card, an organ donation card, that Government Gateway card for your online tax return which always needs a million different passwords, or Ryanair frequent flyer points.

bodies. For example, the EU has competence to set trading rules within the single market, but not to dictate to member states how they should hold their own national elections. Rather like the use of the word 'intelligence' in its espionage sense, 'competence' here leaves itself open to any number of obvious gags about it actually being quite the opposite.

Council of Europe: an organisation for human rights and democracy which has, since its foundation in 1949, produced the European Convention on Human Rights (ECHR) and the European Court of Human Rights in Strasbourg. It is *not* an EU body, though all EU members are also members of it (as are 19 other nations). Brexit does not mean UK withdrawal from the Council of Europe, though of course the UK could also unilaterally decide to leave the Council of Europe too.

Council of the European Union: also known as the Council of Ministers, where government ministers from each member state meet to co-ordinate policies and discuss, amend and adopt laws. The ministers have authority to commit their own governments to actions agreed in these meetings, which makes this (along with the European Parliament) the EU's main decision-making body of the EU. Not to be confused with either the European Council (qv) or the Council of Europe (qv). Or indeed the Privy Council or the Style Council (not qv).

Court of Justice of the European Union (CJEU): ensures that EU law is interpreted and applied in the same way in all member countries, and settles legal disputes between national governments and EU institutions. Individuals, companies or organisations can in some circumstances use the Court to take action against an EU institution for alleged infringements of their rights. Established in 1952, based in Luxembourg, and comprises three courts: the Court of Justice (one judge from each member state and 11 Advocates General), which deals with requests for preliminary rulings from national courts and certain actions for annulment and appeals; the General Court (one judge from each member state), which rules on actions for annulment and deals mainly with competition law, state aid, trade, agriculture, trademarks etc; and the Civil Service Tribunal (seven judges), which rules on disputes between the EU and its staff. If this all sounds complex, that's because the two sets of people who can really obfuscate things are lawyers and EU bureaucrats, so when you get both together it's a black hole of confusion.

Customs union: the EU-wide agreement under which member states (a) remove tariffs on goods traded between each other and (b) levy the same external tariff on goods entering from the rest of the world, no matter which member state they first come through. The customs union is part of the EU, so the UK will leave the customs union when it leaves the EU (though it can of course negotiate a new union between itself and the EU, as indeed Turkey has).

Department for Exiting the European Union (DExEU): the department of the British government responsible for (a) overseeing negotiations to leave the EU and (b) establishing the future relationship between the UK and EU. Created in July 2016 by Theresa May not long after becoming Prime Minister, and headed by David Davis.

Department for International Trade (DIT): the department of the British government responsible for (a) delivering a new trade and investment policy to promote UK business worldwide, (b) negotiating free trade agreements and market access deals with non-EU countries, and (c) facilitating inward and outward investment. Also created in July 2016 by Theresa May, and headed by Liam Fox. Fox, Davis and Foreign Secretary Boris Johnson therefore between them are tasked with delivering Brexit, though their responsibilities vary.[46]

Directive: a legal stricture which is 'binding, as to the result to be achieved, upon each Member State to which it is addressed, but shall leave to the national authorities the choice of form and methods' – that is, the directive sets the end goal and each member state decides how best to get there through 'transposition'.

Euratom:[47] the European Atomic Energy Community which regulates the nuclear industry. Though governed

---

46 This trio is seen by Leave campaigners as the Three Brexiteers, swashbuckling their way through hapless Eurocrats, and by Remainers as a cross between the three Stooges and the *Last of the Summer Wine* trio of Compo, Foggy and Cleggy (not to be confused with staunch Remainer Sir Nick Clegg).

47 Pronounced 'your atom', but not to be confused with 'your mum', long-time insult of choice among certain members of the youth. One is liable to cause a nuclear explosion if used incorrectly. The other is Euratom.

by the EU's institutions, it is a separate legal entity. The UK has announced its intention to withdraw from Euratom as part of the general Brexit process.

European Arrest Warrant: allows one EU member state to arrest and transfer suspects to another.

European Commission: the EU's executive body. Proposes legislation, implements decisions, upholds EU treaties and manages the EU's quotidian business. A European Cabinet, more or less. There are 28 Commissioners in all, one from each member state, and each Commissioner has his or her own specific area of responsibility (the current Commissioner from the UK is Julian King, responsible for the security union). Commissioners are bound by their oath of office to represent the EU as a whole rather than their nation of origin. The Commission employs around 23,000 civil servants and operates in three languages: English, French and German.

European Communities Act (ECA) 1972: the Act of Parliament by which the UK (a) joined the then European Economic Community (EEC), European Coal and Steel Community (ECSC) and the European Atomic Energy Community (Euratom) and (b) legislated for the incorporation of EC (now EU) law into the UK's domestic law. The ECA will be repealed upon leaving the EU by a proposed 'Great Repeal Bill' (qv).

European Convention on Human Rights (ECHR): since this comes from the Council of Europe (qv), this is not an EU document and Brexit will not mean an automatic withdrawal from the ECHR.

European Council: comprises the heads of state/government of the 28 EU member states, along with the European Commission President and the High Representative for Foreign Affairs & Security Policy. Usually meets four times a year, and defines the EU's political direction and policy agenda. The current President of the European Council is Donald Tusk.[48]

European Economic Area (EEA): comprises all 28 EU member states along with Norway, Iceland and Liechtenstein. The three non-EU EEA members apply most EU single market laws, but not in the following areas: most of the Common Agricultural Policy (qv) and Common Fisheries Policy, the customs union, common trade policy, common foreign and security policy, justice and home affairs, and economic and monetary union. EEA members can have input into the development of EU rules, but they do not have a final vote.[49]

European Free Trade Area (EFTA): Norway, Iceland, Liechtenstein and Switzerland – that is, the three non-EU EEA states plus Switzerland, who always have to be different (though their flag's a big plus). Switzerland has a bilateral freedom of movement agreement with the EU,

---

48 Despite his name, neither an elephant nor anything to do with the Fleetwood Mac album.

49 E, E and A are also the kind of low-scoring, useless tiles you have left at the end of a Scrabble game.

allowing EU citizens to live or work in Switzerland. The UK was a founding member of EFTA back in 1960, and could possibly rejoin after leaving the EU (which in turn would give the UK access to EFTA's existing trade agreements, though some renegotiation might be required).[50]

European Parliament (EP): composed of 751 members (MEPs) from the 28 member states. Directly elected every five years, most MEPs are organised into seven parliamentary groups (30 MEPs are unattached). Along with the Council of the European Union (qv), the EP can adopt legislation, control the EU budget and elect the President of the Commission.

European Union (EU): a political and economic union comprising 28 member states, which will soon be 27 (if that wasn't the case, this book wouldn't exist). Established by the Maastricht Treaty of 1992 and updated by the Lisbon Treaty of 2009.[51]

Europol: the EU's law enforcement agency. Facilitates co-operation between member states, provides support for national law enforcement and has data processing and analysing capabilities to help fight organised crime and terrorism.

EUSSR: a portmanteau of 'EU' and 'USSR', used by hardcore Brexiteers who equate the EU with the old

---

50   E, F, T and A are slightly more useful when it comes to topping up your Scrabble score.

51   No country has ever left it to date. Hey, at least we're first at something.

Soviet Union. A superstate comprising many different republics, ruled by faceless bureaucrats and bent on world domination… and the USSR. Joking aside, the comparison is absolutely facile, not to mention insulting to the memory of the millions who died and suffered under the totalitarian Soviet regime. If the bluffer comes across anyone who uses the word 'EUSSR', walk away: not because you won't know more than them (you almost certainly will), but because there's no point trying to bluff someone who thinks this way. Save your breath.

Four freedoms: freedom of movement of people, capital, goods and services. Central to the concept and working of the single market.

Free trade agreement (FTA): an agreement between two or more countries to reduce barriers to trade, such as tariffs, between them. Usually (a) concentrate more on goods than services and (b) don't altogether remove trade barriers to the extent of the single market. Perhaps the best known free trade agreement outside the EU is the North American Free Trade Agreement (NAFTA) between Canada, the USA and Mexico.

'Great Repeal Bill': the legislation which will take effect the day the UK leaves the EU, and will (a) repeal the ECA (qv) and (b) transpose all existing EU legislation into domestic UK law to avoid a legal black hole and prevent disruption. Parliament can then 'amend, repeal and improve' each law as necessary. That should keep them busy, if not quiet, for some time to come.

Hard Brexit: like 'soft Brexit' (qv), not clearly defined, but generally taken as meaning a withdrawal deal which extracts the UK from pretty much all the EU's structures and mechanisms, particularly the single market, the customs union and the European Court of Justice (ECJ), and leaves the UK independent or isolated, depending on your point of view. Hard Brexit would almost certainly involve a short-term economic hit as tariffs are reintroduced and bilateral trade deals negotiated. Those in favour of a hard Brexit think this hit will be worth it compared to the longer-term ability to chart the UK's own economic destiny. Those against it fear that it won't: indeed, that it will be just the start of sustained economic decline.

Miller case: technically 'R (on the application of Miller and Dos Santos) v Secretary of State for Exiting the European Union [2016]', this is the legal case brought by Gina Miller (a private citizen) contending that parliament had to vote on whether or not to enact Article 50, and that the government could not use the royal prerogative in this instance. Miller's claim was upheld by both the High Court and the Supreme Court.

No-deal Brexit: an even harder Brexit than Hard Brexit. Leaving the EU without a withdrawal agreement of any sort, as in 'no deal is better than a bad deal'. In such a scenario, trade would be the least of the problems, as trade between the UK and EU would be covered by WTO rules (qv). The regulatory limbo in other areas would be chaotic (see 'cliff edge' (qv) for examples). And of course a unilateral withdrawal from talks would make any future FTA (qv) harder to achieve.

Non-tariff barrier: obstacles to trade which aren't directly-levied tariffs. Examples include border checks, differences in regulatory regimes, language difficulties, paperwork, dispute resolution mechanisms, and so on. Not universally accepted as such: as with the old terrorist/freedom fighter dichotomy, one person's red tape can be another's legal safeguards, and one person's healthandsafetygonemad can be another's vital security measures.

Red, white and blue Brexit: Theresa May's description of the kind of Brexit she wanted to achieve, but a description on which she has never enlarged. Presumably means a Brexit which suits the UK rather than any of the other 36 countries whose flags have those same three colours, including seven in the EU (plus, of course, Russia and the USA). Maybe she meant the Cook Islands. Or the Faroe Islands. Probably the Cook Islands, on reflection. Theresa, can you clarify? Theresa?

Regulation: an EU law which applies directly and uniformly in all member states, without the need for further national implementing measures. 'A regulation shall have general application. It shall be binding in its entirety and directly applicable in all Member States' says the legalese.

Reste à liquider:[52] the total of the UK's outstanding financial commitments to the EU (such as budget payments signed off but not yet made). The amount for which Boris Johnson said the EU could 'go whistle'. Coincidentally, the same amount which Theresa May has now agreed to pay round about £50bn for.

Single market: the removal of tariffs and regulatory barriers to trade between the 28 member states of the EU. Almost complete in terms of goods, though not when it comes to services. The largest and most comprehensive free trade area in the world. Based on the 'four freedoms' (qv).

Smooth Brexit: an orderly process of withdrawal with no obstacles or drama along the way. See also 'flying pigs' (not qv).

Soft Brexit: like Hard Brexit (qv), not rigidly defined, but generally accepted as meaning the maintenance of as close and intertwined a relationship with the EU as possible, perhaps as a member of the EEA (qv) and/or EFTA (qv). Easier to justify economically than politically, as would minimise the economic shock associated with leaving the EU but would also (a) constrain the UK's ability to negotiate new trade agreements with non-EU countries and (b) require concessions on free movement, ECJ jurisdiction and budget payments. Hardcore Brexiteers do not consider a soft Brexit as proper Brexit.

---

52 Not to be confused with the amount of wine left in the bottle at the end of an evening, and it would be such a waste not to finish it off, wouldn't it? See *The Bluffer's Guide To Wine*.

Sovereignty: the authority of a state to govern itself and determine its own laws and policies. In the UK, sovereignty rests with parliament (more specifically the crown-in-parliament, i.e. the monarch acting on parliamentary advice), meaning that parliament is the highest source of authority and can make laws without restriction. The primacy of EU law in the UK legislature since 1972 is, in terms of sovereignty, either an abdication of power to Brussels (Leave) or a voluntary pooling of authority in certain areas which doesn't affect the issues which most countries regard as the 'spine' of their sovereignty (defence, taxation, elections etc.)

Super qualified majority: the margin which will be needed for the EU to agree any Brexit withdrawal agreement. Defined in this instance as at least 72% of the participating members of the EU Council which in turn comprise at least 65% of the population of those member states (to prevent an instance, no matter how unlikely, where lots of smaller countries voted in favour but a few larger countries such as France and Germany voted against). Not to be confused with: Super Furry Animals, Super Mario, supercalifragilisticexpialidocious or, if you're a Caledonian Thistle supporter, SUPERCALLYGOBALLISTICCELTICAREATROCIOUS.

Tariff: a tax levied on a product entering a country, paid by the importer to the government and usually passed onto the customer. Can be either *ad valorem* (a percentage of the goods' value) or specific (a fixed amount per measure of weight/volume).

Transition: the process of moving from EU membership to non-EU membership. A period required for government departments, businesses etc to make arrangements for new regulatory requirements. Likely to be 21 months, from the day the UK officially leaves the EU (29 March 2019) to the day the EU's seven-year budget period ends (31 December 2020.)[53]

United Kingdom Permanent Representation to the European Union (UKRep): the team which represents the UK in all EU negotiations (not just Brexit). Team members have been transferred or seconded from more than 20 UK government departments. Led by Sir Tim Barrow.[54]

World Trade Organisation (WTO): an organisation comprising 164 member countries which sets the international frameworks governing trade in goods and services. WTO rules are universal: a country which extends benefits under the rules to another country must then do so for every country (the 'most favoured nation' (MFN) rule). WTO rules are more prohibitive than specific bilateral and multilateral treaties: if the UK were therefore to trade with the EU under WTO rules (the default position in the event of no deal), it would face substantial tariff barriers.

---

53   Britain will therefore see in 2021 in the time-honoured fashion: by waking up with an emperor-sized hangover and a vague memory of having done something seismic the night before.

54   Whose nickname, rather annoyingly, doesn't seem to be 'Wheel'.